P9-CFA-947

3 1611 00178 4617

97410

97410
DA   Rickword, Edgell.
535   Radical squibs
.R53   & loyal
1971b   ripostes;
            satirical ...

UNIVERSITY LIBRARY
Governors State University
Park Forest South, Il. 60466
WITHDRAWN

Radical Squibs

&

Loyal Ripostes

Satirical Pamphlets of the Regency Period, 1819–1821
Illustrated by George Cruikshank and others

Selected and annotated by
EDGELL RICKWORD

BARNES & NOBLE, Inc.
NEW YORK
PUBLISHERS & BOOKSELLERS SINCE 1873

UNIVERSITY LIBRARY
GOVERNORS STATE UNIVERSITY
PARK FOREST SOUTH, ILL.

For Beatrix

The engraving on the title page depicts
Hone and Cruikshank collaborating on a squib
(from the title-page of Hone's *Facetiae
and Miscellanies*, 1827)

© 1971, Edgell Rickword

First published in the United States 1971
by Barnes & Noble, Inc.

ISBN 389 04084 3

All rights reserved

Printed in Great Britain

Contents

Acknowledgements

Works consulted include:

Aspinall, A. *Politics and the Press, 1780–1850* 1949

Cohn, A. M. *George Cruikshank, a Catalogue Raisonné of the Work executed, 1806–1877* 1924

Gentleman's Magazine: February 1843 (obituary article)

George, Dr. D. M. *Catalogue of Political and Personal Satires preserved in the Department of Prints and Drawings, British Museum* Vols. 7–10

Hackwood, F. W. *The Life and Times of William Hone* 1912 (includes the only printing of Hone's autobiographical fragment)

Madden, R. R. *The United Irishmen: Series Three* 1860 (2nd ed.)

Rolleston, F. *Some account of the conversion of the late William Hone. With further particulars of his life and extracts from his correspondence* 1853

The Early Life and Conversion of William Hone (Senior), edited by his Son 1841

Thompson, E. P. *The Making of the English Working Class* 1963

Watkins, John *Life, Poetry, and Letters of Ebenezer Elliott, the Corn-Law Rhymer. With an abstract of his politics* 1850

Wickwar, W. H. *The Struggle for the Freedom of the Press, 1819–1832* 1928

DA
535
.R53
1971b

Foreword

There has been no new edition of any of these pamphlets since they were originally issued. A few of the woodcuts have been individually reproduced, with much loss of quality; and being seen out of context their singular appositeness is altogether lost. George Cruikshank, in the years of his collaboration with William Hone, designed and cut more than 150 blocks for his publications. This pamphleteering provided a very apt field for the development of Cruikshank's vision and skill, in the course of which he utterly transcended the mundane requirements of political partisanship. Even an artist so prolific as he was must benefit from having this fecund period of his creative life restored to general appreciation, from which it has been unaccountably withheld for a very long while.

At the same time a measure of justice is repaid to his friend and mentor, William Hone, whose ready humour and wide acquaintance with the hearty traditions of our popular culture stimulated the imagination of the younger man. And these pamphlets, so contemptuously defiant of their powerful adversaries, owed their immunity from prosecution to the courageous defence which Hone had earlier maintained against the most formidable judges who ever tried a poor man. His acquittal made him a popular hero.

Hone's sudden return to the attack, two years after his legal triumph, caught the self-styled Loyalists unawares. New Acts had just been passed in Parliament to prevent this very thing. *The Political House that Jack Built* was like a shrapnel barrage, striking from all directions. The Loyalists were hard put to it to mount a counter-attack; the appeal of their pamphlets was limited and none of them caught the popular fancy. But they provide valuable evidence of the frame of mind with which the Radicals had to reckon, an unreasoning hostility to every innovation which appeared to threaten the inbred privileges of an effete caste.

Some account of the background and career of the man whose initial protest was responsible for this richly entertaining interlude, will serve to bring much disparate material into focus. William Hone's apparently trivial misdemeanours forced great issues into the open. The laughter his squibs generated shook to its foundations the graceful façade of the Age of Elegance.

E.R. May 1970

William Hone 1780–1842 by G. Patten (National Portrait Gallery)

WILLIAM HONE

I *Antecedents of a Parodist*

My right hon. Friend [William Windham] has called me a counsel for the Press . . . I am glad of the appellation. But I confess that I was a good deal surprised when he put in his claim to a share of the distinction. He has questioned . . . the use of the liberty of the Press! Can he have been serious? Give me but the liberty of the Press, and I will give to the Minister a venal House of Peers—I will give him a corrupt and servile House of Commons; I will give him the full swing of the patronage of office—I will give him the whole host of ministerial influence; . . . And after, armed with the liberty of the Press, I will go forth with that mightier engine; I will shake down from its height corruption, and bury it beneath the ruins of the abuses it was meant to shelter.

> *R. B. Sheridan, on a Motion to exclude Strangers, including Press reporters, from the House. February 1810.*

The subject of these satires is not, as might have been assumed from the accompanying illustrations, the moral laxity of the Prince of Wales and the indiscretions of his royal Consort, Caroline of Brunswick. It is not even about the threat, or the desirability, of Revolution. It is really about the extension of the Parliamentary Franchise, Trial by Jury, and the Liberty of the Press. The adultery and gourmandising are only the condiments to make those illustrious abstractions palatable.

The waste and extravagance, the high jinks in court circles, the giddy carnival of Regency society, were not the primary cause of the prevalent distress in Britain. No one knew the complete answer to it and this is no place to attempt it. But there was a spirit abroad which spread confidence that an answer was to be found. Some thought, following Major Cartwright, that a return to Anglo-Saxon institutions was the answer; others, more numerous, that the French had made a good start towards it in 1789. These notions, especially the second, produced in the Administration a mindless reaction. Though twenty years' expenditure of blood and wealth had at last replaced a Bourbon on the throne of France and restored the hegemony of Legitimacy and the Roman Catholic church over all of Western Europe, the horrid disease of 'Jacobinism' showed renewed virulence in Britain.

Hence a policy of repression and provocation was resorted to by the successors of William Pitt and Edmund Burke, though they lacked both the talents of the one and the eloquence of the other. But they provided at least a rich heritage of caricature for their posterity. To this Hone and Cruikshank made the most significant contribution.

There is not much material for an account of Hone's early life, beyond what he has himself told us in some reminiscences of his first twenty years. He was born in Bath, but London was essentially his home ground, for his parents returned there shortly after his birth, and all his active life was passed there. His paternal grandfather had farmed land at Ripley, in Sussex, and here, at Homewood Farm, his father had spent his childhood. Hone the younger retained a strong sense of family relationship, and when he was nearing sixty made a pilgrimage to Ripley, where he gathered up such scanty crumbs regarding his grandfather as the memory of the parish clerk could call up, or fabricate.

The father was apprenticed when about fifteen to a London attorney. Apprenticeship was often little better than slavery at the time, and this master, who had several pupils, starved them for good measure. By sheer luck, they found a sympathetic lawyer, who advised them to appeal against their master, and sent them to a humane magistrate, who put an end to their bondage by cancelling their indentures.

Emancipation did little to advance William Hone's prospects. He fell in with a bohemian set, which was not surprising, as he had lodgings near Soho. He had been brought up a Dissenter, and so acquired a more than usual introspectiveness and awareness of conscience. He even, as his son was to do, composed a fragment of autobiography, up till the time of his marriage. From this we find that as a Dissenter he had imbibed strong principles, of an intensity which goes back to the sectaries of the Civil War, at least. He might have found a natural place in Ephraim Pagitt's *Heresiagraphie*.

That each of these William Hones should write an account of his own early life is only one of a number of traits which shows that they had some fundamental characteristics in common. They each married the daughter of their landlady—a flight into the nearest refuge? The father was certainly neurotic, the son better balanced, but with a religious streak never far below the surface. Both were for a time, in their teens, obsessed with the theatre, a very usual trait in young men at the time, but in the father's case showing pathological symptoms. He records how, through an older friend, he made acquaintance with a group of people in show-business, one of whom was

Moses Kean, the celebrated theatrical imitator, and his chief companions were Mr. John Bannister and others in that line. These persons, in a measure, became my associates, with whom I repeatedly rehearsed parts of plays, and got such a love for the stage that I was play-mad. It was settled by us that I should go on the stage, but God had planned otherwise. In the midst of my play-house work, and about the time of my intended first appearance at the Haymarket Theatre, such a strange thing happened as completely struck me dead to the least desire for reading a play or attempting to see one. One evening, on going to the Haymarket Theatre as usual, and taking my seat in the pit, I waited anxiously for the play to commence, but when the actors appeared, each seemed to my view, in the hideous shape of a devil, which so affrighted me that I instantly rushed out with all possible speed. Thus was I chased from the service of Satan in his playhouse work; but although scared from that part of his service, he still kept possession of his palace, and his goods were yet in peace.

Still a deeper unrest possessed him: 'I had become so opposed to a married life that I resolutely determined to destroy my constitution in a perpetual round of dissipation'. The need for a means of livelihood induced him to move from London to Bath, where there was a connection of his family's who might perhaps be able to place him in a situation. After an arduous journey, a flight, as it seemed, he arrived in Bath practically penniless and suffered a complete mental and physical breakdown. Providentially, a kind-hearted landlady succoured him, and her daughter's ministrations so softened his resolution against matrimony, that his first child and son was born in Bath, and received his father's name.

The married state had not eradicated the elder Hone's religious orientation. He regarded the Bible as the source of all essential knowledge and abhorred all ritual and ceremonies. It was from his mother that the young William derived the warmth of his nature, and at an early age he became estranged from his father's sectarian exclusiveness. He had heard his father speak of John Wesley as 'the child of the devil', and it so happened that Wesley, then in extreme old age, came to their house to visit an old dame who had taught William, and been very kind to him. She was now dying and Wesley had come to minister to her. The small boy peeped at the visitor through the bannisters, expecting to see the hairy legs of a devil. But Wesley's 'angelic expression' and gentle smile so enraptured the frightened child that 'from that hour I never believed anything my father said or anything I heard at chapel.'

It will be noticed as a characteristic of the pamphlets whose texts were composed by Hone, that they are interspersed with very numerous quotations, from an astonishing variety of sources and generally applied with immediate relevance. This stems from a magnetic attraction to print and no doubt a photographic memory. As he tells us:

I was in the habit of making my own every bit of printed and written paper, whether from cheese-mongers or other shops, and one day met with an old printed leaf, which seemed to be part of an energetic defence of some man. I could not discover who he was, nor could my father. . . . At last I obtained the information from a bookseller who possessed a copy of the book. It was the *Trial of John Lilburne.* . . . By patience, industry and extraordinary management I accumulated half-a-crown—I had for some time improved my resources by the disposal of toys and boxes which I made of card, and I bought the book.

Though he was only eleven at the time, 'No book', he says, 'since the *Pilgrim's Progress*, had so rivetted me. I felt all Lilburne's indignant feelings, admired his undaunted spirit, rejoiced at his acquittal, and detested Cromwell as a tyrant for causing him to be carried back to the Tower, after the Jury had pronounced him to be free of the charge [of treason].' He says that this reading aroused within him new feelings, and a desire to study Constitutional Law. A precocious youngster! It would not be fanciful, though, to believe that the recalling of this strong impression of Lilburne's fortitude would have revived his flagging energies during his own marathon trials.

But he records an even earlier political experience, felt on the nerves rather than the understanding, for he was only nine years and a month old at the time.

In July 1789, a boy whom I knew suddenly stopped me in Hand Court, Holborn, from driving my hoop, and with mysterious looks and voice he said: 'There's a revolution in France.' Little instructed, the word 'Revolution' was new to me; I stared at him and enquired, 'What's a revolution?' 'Why, the French people in Paris have taken the Bastille, and hung the Governor, and let loose all the prisoners, and pulled the Bastille down to the ground.'

Hone's mother was a woman of character, with ideas of her own. She was an admirer of the character of Cromwell. When the National Assembly declared war on the counter-revolutionary Powers, she began to take in a daily newspaper. With the additional assistance of the propaganda issued by the 'Association for preserving Liberty and Property against Republicans and Levellers' young William Hone concocted a poem which shows him to have been still under the spell of 'constitutionalism'. It was called The Contrast and, when printed on a quarter-sheet of paper, a copy was sent to the Association named, 'which procured me a flattering letter of thanks from the Secretary'. It is amusing to find the future Radical, bugbear of all Loyalists, so fluent in the manipulation of conservative stereotypes:

> Come Britons, unite, and in one Common Cause
> Stand up in defence of King, Liberty, Laws,
> And rejoice that we've got such a good Constitution,
> And down with the barbarous French Revolution!
>
> There's Egalité Marat and famous Tom Paine
> Had best stay where they are and not come here to reign . . .

4

II *Rough Times to Grow Up in*

'So barbarous were some of the deeds done in that time in the name of law, and so painful was the impression which they made on me when I was about sixteen years old, that I should certainly have emigrated to the United States had I possessed sufficient funds for that purpose; nor should I, I fear, have been very scrupulous as to the means of obtaining them. . . .' Thus wrote Ebenezer Elliott, later known as the Corn-Law Rhymer, born a year after Hone and brought up in the Yorkshire countryside, though in the proximity of an iron-foundry. Elliott's father, who managed the foundry, was a Dissenter, as Hone's was; but the iron-master belonged to a more extreme sect. He was an ultra-Calvinist, and would preach in his sermons of a hell 'hung round with span-long children'. His political views were considered ultra-Radical; 'he delighted to declaim on the virtues of slandered Cromwell and of Washington the rebel'. So when the local Yeomanry took the fancy to back their horses so as to break the windows of this Jacobin's office, he knew he would get no redress from the law.

This 'white terror' was nation-wide in the seventeen-nineties, administered heartily by the magistrates if there was a shadow of a legal excuse; otherwise, where no legal pretext could be invoked, by a sort of lynch- or mob-law. The first was well exemplified by the trial, in Edinburgh, of the delegates from the London Corresponding Society to the Scottish Convention in 1794, where sentences to long periods of transportation were passed down. Of the second sort, the 'Church and King' mob which in 1792 destroyed Joseph Priestley's library and laboratory in Birmingham was typical.

So when young Hone, in his fifteenth year, began attending lectures in London given under the auspices, more or less disguised, of the London Corresponding Society, he was in danger of incrimination under the panic laws of the Pitt Administration. Lurking around there were, no doubt, sinister individuals who would not hesitate to take advantage of his youth to lure him within the 'statute's iron jaws'.

I have quoted those two outstanding examples to illustrate the generalised, ubiquitous character of the terror. This has been played down by all the 'impartial' historians who, once praised for presenting a 'balanced view', have now been succeeded by a school which does not eschew a dynamic interpretation. Contemporary accounts of the conditions under which 'justice' was administered in the period we have here destroy any respect for apologists of the regime. In the House of Correction in Cold Bath Fields, not a mile from where Hone was living, conditions amounted to nothing better than continual torture. Money could sometimes procure an amelioration of prison conditions, and collections were often made to assist prisoners in this way, but this was a mere palliative. Young Hone grew up in this very tense atmosphere, which reached the extreme of dramatic suspense when the leaders of the London Corresponding Society were put on trial for their lives at the Old Bailey in October, 1794. Huge meetings called by the Society must have attracted the boy whose mind had been set agog by Lilburne's defiance of a tyrannical government. But it is disappointing to find that the reaction against intervention in politics which overtook Hone in middle life inhibited him from giving a fuller account of his behaviour in those days. He leaves us only the barest record in his 'Memoir':

When about sixteen I became a member of the London Corresponding Society, very much to the distress of my Father. My connection with that and other debating societies completed the mischief. . . . I became a convert to this wretch-making New Philosophy as it was then called, which Mr. Robert Owen has since revised and systematically attempted to diffuse, under the name of 'Socialism'.

In the 1790s it must have been Godwinian anarchism and a smattering of materialism which seduced him, not socialism. However, when he heard Godwin lecture he was rather discouraged by the aridity of the philosopher's discourse. A later acquaintance of Hone's, John Britton, antiquarian and topographer (who speaks kindly of him in his *Auto-Biography*), has this to say of the many debating societies which were

prevalent and popular in the last five years of the eighteenth century, and indeed for some years after. . . . Political and religious subjects were prohibited in most of these bodies; but the public events of that remarkable era were great and exciting; and other societies were formed in which they were freely and critically discussed. The momentous French Revolution unhinged and disorganised the whole of the civilised world. . . . Many of the public debating societies were formed and governed by speculating and hackneyed orators, who derived pay and profit from admission fees paid at the doors. . . . One of the most active and popular of the managers and proprietors of these societies was John Gale Jones, a noted mob-orator, of great fluency of speech, though cautious in his language . . .

This Jones was one of the leading members of the London Corresponding Society, and published an account of his lecture tour through the Medway towns in 1796. This tour provided evidence of the activity of political discussion in the district. Ironically, it was to Chatham that William Hone, senior, banished his son to remove him from noxious influences. When young Hone returned to London in the late 'nineties he had become, he says, 'not merely a Deist but an Atheist'.

Deism and materialism were much under discussion. Richard Carlile was not yet publishing heretical tracts, but D. I. Eaton had anticipated him, and published the first part of Paine's *Age of Reason* in 1795. Translations (some of them abridgements) of the French *philosophes*, Rousseau, Voltaire, Helvétius, Diderot, Volney, d'Holbach were in circulation from the 'eighties onwards.

III *High Aims, for a small Bookseller*

When Hone returned to London from Chatham he was approaching eighteen. Besides an amiable character, ready wit and a fund of miscellaneous information, he had no qualifications for a career. He took lodgings in Lambeth and continued for a time as a lawyer's clerk. On Sundays he attended Chapel, finding that his loss of any religious conviction had left him with a sense of frustration. He studied the Bible methodically, endeavouring to extract from it an ethical basis of conduct, free from any transcendentalism. Although not satisfied, he seems for the time being to have settled for a kind of altruism. Then he fell in love with his landlady's daughter, married her, and opened a small bookshop with a library and stationery counter. It was soon made clear that, whatever his other talents, he had no business sense. He was fortunate in his choice of a wife, and their affection served to sustain them through a life-time of insolvency and the cares of a large family. During the invasion threat of 1805–6 he joined the Prince of Wales' Volunteer Corps. Lambeth having proved a bad spot for their sort of trade, they moved to St. Martin's Lane, where they found a better type of customer, among them a famous collector, Sir Charles Townley, and Hone further extended his knowledge of antiquities and fine prints. But always some contretemps seemed to happen to him and worsen an already precarious situation— the lease of the premises was shorter than he had been led to believe, and this necessitated the expense of another move.

At some time before his marriage, when he was attending meetings of the London Corresponding Society, he made the acquaintance of John Bone, a leading member of it and for a time its Secretary. He was a popular speaker, and sentenced to a term of imprisonment towards the end of the century. He is described as a bookseller, which must have led to closer contact with Hone. At any rate, they were involved in a joint enterprise, about which we find the earliest entry in Hone's bibliography, in the British Museum Catalogue:

> The Rules and Regulations of an Institute called
> Tranquillity, (with a prefatory address by W. Hone)
> 1807

The address is a prophetic warning of the misery of poverty in old age and a eulogy of the magic remedy now offered, regular saving out of current earnings.

An emotional passage in Hone's *Third Trial* gives an insight into the high expectations with which he endeavoured to launch this now discredited engine:

I attempted, in conjunction with a friend, who originated the plan, to establish something of an institution similar to the saving-banks that are now so general. There was a number associated for this purpose and I was their secretary. Our object was to get the patronage of ministers for our scheme. Mr. Fox was then in power. It was the Whig Administration. We hoped to throw a grain into the earth which would become a great tree—in other hands it has succeeded. It was very Quixotic—we were mad; mad because we supposed it possible, if an intention were good, that it would therefore be carried into effect, but we met with that trifling and delaying of hope that makes the heart sick.

Quixotic Hone remained to the end, at least if that means a disregard of the consequences for himself in which an unselfish object might involve him.

Another nine or ten years were to pass in enterprises which by one calamitous accident or another, fire, theft or commercial depression, pushed him nearer to the gutter. And his family continued to increase. He wrote reviews for the *Ladies Magazine*, edited the *Critical Review* for six months, edited *Shaw's Gardener* and indexed *Froissart*, but barely kept his head above water. At one point he was elected Trade Auctioneer to the booksellers who made a business of speculative remaindering. But as Britton remarks: 'He was irregular in his accounts, whence arose many embarrassments in after life.'

VI *Publisher on a Shoe-string*

By his own reckoning, William Hone began publishing in the second quarter of 1815. This is clearly stated in his weekly *The Reformists' Register*, 25 October 1817, where he writes:

It is now two years and a half since I commenced to publish; in the course of which time I have issued upwards of one hundred and thirty pieces, chiefly of my own production. Not a week has elapsed during that period, without my having compiled or written something; but whether it were prose or verse, or 'grave, or gay, or lively, or severe', I console myself with the reflection that, amidst all I have put on paper there is
>   'Not one immoral, one indecent thought,
>   One line which, dying, I would wish to blot.'
Nor can there be found a single paragraph, or even sentence, of a profane or irreligious tendency in any of my publications. With a lively conception of wit, and an irresistible propensity to humour, I have likewise so profound a regard for the well-being of society, and so great a reverence for public morals, that I know of no temptation capable of inducing me to pen a line injurious to social happiness, or offensive to private virtue.

It will be noticed that this disclaimer does not include the susceptibilities of politicians. Hone must have been more unsophisticated than one need believe him to have been, if he really did not intend most of his publications to be highly offensive to this class of persons. But it is not impossible that his enjoyment of his own satiric excursions may have dimmed his apprehension of the risks involved at a time of highly inflamed antagonisms.

With the exception of a few pamphlets motivated towards humanitarian ends—the ill-treatment of lunatics, the abuse of blood money, the dangers of accepting circumstantial evidence—his publishing output proclaimed a political stance of unqualified hostility to the measures, policies and principles of the Government. At the period from which Hones dates the commencement of his publishing venture, his living conditions had fallen to a level hardly short of destitution. He had some kind of accommodation in or near Old Bailey, but was without means to furnish more than one room. His wife and four of their seven children lodged here, three children being taken care of by their mother's mother in Lambeth. He also had lock-up premises at 55 Fleet Street, with a shop-window only three feet wide. From this address he issued his own earliest publications and also carried a small stock of books, pamphlets and journals. The shop was three times broken into and ransacked. It is not surprising that with all this hardship and anxiety he should have suffered what he calls an attack of apoplexy.

Hone did not, as an early biographer alleged, become a muckraker, publishing accounts of scandalous law-suits or bloody crimes. Most of his non-satirical output has a serious intention. He began with very short items, selling at twopence to sixpence each. From the outset he realised the increase of impact to be obtained from the association of image and letterpress, a tradition then very much alive among the purveyors of demotic literature, in which Seven Dials was most prolific.

Amongst the earliest productions of his new enterprise is a short series of broadsides closely related to the political climate following the escape of Napoleon from Elba. These reflect the views of the Parliamentary opposition and also that expressed in a Resolution of the Common Hall of the City of London advocating a policy of peace with Napoleon. The earliest of these, *Buonaparte-phobia*, is the one which introduced a famous nonentity who was to figure prominently among the ranks of the puppets which Hone aligned as targets for the exercise of his satiric marksmanship. It was here that John Stoddard, leader-writer and later editor of *The Times*, was christened Dr. Slop. The intemperate language and ultra-royalism Hone castigated led to a fall in the circulation and influence of *The Times*, and was amongst the reasons for his dismissal at the end of 1816. Whereupon he founded the *New Times* (*Slop-Pail* is Hone's descriptive term for it) with a regular Government subsidy. Hone's seminal broadside has the lay-out of a newspaper, with the appropriate but tongue-twisting title of *Buonaparte-phobia, or Cursing made easy to the meanest Capacity.* It parodies Sterne, in the form of a dialogue between Dr. Slop, My Uncle Toby and My Father. The visual factor is supplied by a fine engraving of David's portrait of Napoleon as he appeared on his return from Elba. The broadside was reprinted with a new Preface in 1820 in octavo format.

Hone's next broadside, *The King's Statue, at Guildhall,* began that long and productive collaboration with George Cruikshank which developed a new form of caricature and illustrative style. The artist was twelve years younger than his publisher, so that there was something of the elder and younger brother in their relationship. There was also warm friendship. Cruikshank was twenty-three or twenty-four and had already more than ten years experience as a professional caricaturist and engraver, the various techniques of the trade having been acquired at a very early age through assisting in the work-room of his father, Isaac Cruikshank. George's headpiece to this broadside depicted the unveiling or first public display of Chantrey's recent statue of George III. The leading members of the Cabinet, the Lord Mayor and other high functionaries are depicted in various postures. Sidmouth 'The Doctor' is already identified by the clyster pipe protruding from his pocket, and Lord Ellenborough, prophetically anticipating his downfall at Hone's trial two years later, has fallen flat on his face. The letterpress, by Hone, attacks the policy of redistributing the French conquests in Europe, and mocks the ludicrous re-enactment of Louis XVIII's re-enthronement.

Cruikshank had now succeeded Rowlandson as the leading political caricaturist. His collaboration can certainly not have recommended Hone to any of the security corps who kept a watch on manifestations of radical opinion, for Cruikshank had already devised some of the cruellest fantasies deriving from the Prince's amorous foibles. One of them was incited by Charles Lamb's squib on the princely obesity, *The Triumph of the Whale.*

The remaining designs of 1815 are masterpieces of acidic comment on the practical consequences of the deliberations of the allied plenipotenaries exerted at their long and expensive Congress at Vienna. The earliest may be an adaptation of a French print (it could have circulated only surreptitiously), *Louis XVIII climbing the Mât de Cocagne.* Hone's advertisement on the wrapper of a later publication, after the title, continues 'or soaped pole to bear off the Imperial crown. This *celebrated caricature* privately circulated at Paris, contains 15 Distinguished Characters, Views of St. Helena, the Massacres at Nismes etc.' The sardonic snatches of dialogue between the distinguished figures are no doubt by Hone. Another print, *Fast Colours*, portrays a grotesque Louis XVIII as an old woman at a wash-tub, over the side of which hangs a tricolour. As time proved, the forcible re-imposition of a Bourbon *pur sang* could not eliminate the achievements of the Revolution. The last caricature for 1815 had the title, *Afterpeace [sic] to the Tragedy of Waterloo* and is a variation on the theme of France's subjugation to the Allies.

These few publications cannot have done much to relieve the necessities of a man with a wife and seven children, and of the pamphlets that may be attributed to this year's output, only one made a substantial contribution towards the family's elementary requirements. It was the single occasion on which Hone's fundamental humanitarian instincts, which more often than not occupied his time and labour when he could ill afford it, brought him a commercial profit. It was inspired by deep pity for the fate of a young servant girl, sentenced to death for poisoning her master, mistress and their children. The trial had excited much interest, and so many doubts had been thrown on the conclusiveness of the evidence that a reprieve had been expected. It was not granted. By an intervention of Providence, as it seemed afterwards, Hone was caught in the crowd outside Newgate at the time of the girl's execution. Years afterwards he described the scene and the chain of events which unexpectedly followed. I quote at length, as the disjointed narration as reported by Mrs. Rolleston conveys a sense of actuality:

I was going down Newgate street on some business of my own. I got into an immense crowd, that carried me along with them against my will; at length I found myself under the gallows where Eliza Fenning was to be hanged. I had the greatest horror of witnessing an execution, and of this in particular, a young girl, and for the murder of a whole family; but I could not help myself; I was closely wedged in; she was brought out; I saw nothing but I heard all; I heard her protesting her innocence—I heard the prayer— I could hear no more. I stopped my ears, and knew nothing else till I found myself in the middle of the dispersing crowd, and far from the dreadful spot. I made my way to the house of a bookseller, with whom I was very intimate. I asked for a glass of water; I sat down, and told him where I had been; saying, 'that unhappy girl Eliza Fenning has died with a lie in her mouth.' 'Friend Hone', replied he, 'she is with her Almighty Father; I have visited her in prison, so have many of my friends, and we are satisfied of her innocence.' I was up immediately; 'why then has she been executed?' 'We made every possible exertion to save her life,' replied he, 'but we were not listened to.' 'The public must be roused about it,' said I. 'You are the man to do it,' returned he; (I think Mr. Hone said, he offered to print for him what he would write. He went on,) 'I took lodgings away from my family, for I could do nothing among them; and for three weeks I was wholly engrossed with the case of Eliza Fenning. At that time we had a little bookseller's shop; the early coaches used to call for the Sunday papers; (I did not then know the value of the sabbath,) and they took any little squibs of the day that I got for them. On the fourth Saturday, in the dusk of the evening, my wife came in. I said 'sit down and be quiet, I am writing, I cannot speak to you at present;' there she sat in silence, and I wrote on. At last she said, 'Father, the children have no bread,—there is no money for the papers to-morrow morning.' 'Go home,' said I, 'and I will bring you the money.' She went, but I had no idea where to get it; I had not a sixpence. I went to the closet where I kept what I had to eat; I had been living chiefly on tea; there was nothing there but a stale crust of bread. I eat my bread and drank my water, and went off to my friend the bookseller. I went up to him, 'you must lend me four pounds.' 'I shall do no such thing.' '*You must*.' 'What should I do that for?' 'My children are starving—you have made me neglect my family.'—So he gave me the money; I put it up safely, and set off home. As I went through the turnstile into Lincoln's inn fields, there was a pastry-cook's shop lighted up. I stood looking at the things, and thinking of my bread and water, and of the old philosopher, and saying with him, how many things are there here, that I have no occasion for! The play bills stuck up in large red letters caught my eye; 'The Maid and the Magpie, repeated with unbounded applause to overflowing houses.' An idea flashed upon my mind;—I changed one of my notes and went to the play in the pit, and saw the Maid and the Magpie. I went home and said to my wife, give me a pair of candles and snuffers, up stairs, and send for George Cruikshank. He came; I said 'make me a cut of a Magpie hung by the neck to the gallows'—and I put my head on one side, and looked as like a dying Magpie as I could. I did not write, I walked, to my printer's, and by six o'clock in the morning, the Maid and the Magpie was completed; a thousand struck off. Cruikshank was ready with the frontispiece, and my wife sewed them. When the coaches drove up for the newspapers, we were ready with our pamphlets: 'will you have this? How many? 'Half a hundred'— 'a hundred': —so we effectually roused the public to the case of Eliza Fenning; and my family lived four months on the Maid and the Magpie.

The Maid and the Magpye, or, *Which was the thief?* was a new melodrama (adapted from the French) which had opened at the Lyceum Theatre on August 28th. I have not read it, nor been able to find a copy of Hone's pamphlet. But one presumes that the relevance of the play was due to a chain of circumstantial evidence which linked the maid to the crime the magpie had committed.

To subsist for four months on the sales of a sixpenny pamphlet argues that the circulation of it was truly tremendous, or that the standard of living it supported was not far removed from destitution. Of course there were other small sources of income, the odd shillings that would accrue from the wholesaler's discount on the country orders he supplied from other publishers, and he may have had a slightly more substantial return from the agency for the *Traveller* newspaper which he is stated by John Britton to have published. But the situation must have been very distressing, and only a build-up of his publishing list in a short time and at small outlay could render his business self-supporting. By 1817 he had titles amounting to around fifty under his imprint, many of which had been devised or compiled by himself. Few cost as much as a shilling, none more than 6s. 6d. Clearly a lot of work must have been involved for a return that was at best moderate.

One of the more expensive items may be noted. This was an edition of *Wat Tyler*, the dramatic poem written by Robert Southey in his early days when he was a republican and egalitarian. He had been reckoned little better than a Jacobin in the estimation of George Canning, who however had supported his elevation to the post of Poet Laureate. The piece was widely pirated, as in spite of seeking an injunction against its publication Southey was non-suited; the Bench, in the person of Chief Justice Ellenborough, held that the work was seditious and hence outside the protection of the law.

Several publishers took advantage of this farcical situation, to their good profit. Hone's edition however claims a superior interest, since it carries a 'Preface suitable to recent Circumstances'. In other words, Hone had persuaded William Hazlitt to allow him to reprint the very pungent considerations he had devoted to the ex-Pantisocrat in the pages of the *Examiner*. This is the earliest indication, I think, that Hone was in personal contact with that very gifted and courageous group which John and Leigh Hunt had gathered round their consistently democratic journal. It is not to be supposed that the Cabinet was concerned about the Laureate's wounded feeling, but this was certainly another black mark against Hone's name.

More serious were three broadsides, coloured caricatures by Cruikshank.[1] The Regent was notoriously sensitive to ridicule directed at any particularities of the royal person. Now, he had been placed in a very vulnerable situation by a gift offered him ceremoniously by his comrade-in-arms, Ferdinand of Spain, to commemorate their joint triumph over the tyrant and usurper Buonaparte. This gift was a tremendous cannon, or rather mortar, known at the time as a 'bomb'. It was perhaps the most malicious offering that an enemy could have thought of, let alone an ally. The Thing[2] was very difficult to transport and it had arrived without any mounting or carriage. Moreover, the word we now pronounce *bomm* was at that time sounded *bumm*.

Ferdinand was especially obnoxious to British public opinion: as a monument of papist superstition (he is supposed to have spent much

---

[1] The titles were: *Hone's View of the Regent's Bomb, now uncovered for the gratification of the Public*; *Saluting the R----t's Bomb uncovered on his Birthday*; *The Yacht for the R----t's B-m-*. All have verses by Hone elaborating or explicating the jests.

[2] 'Thing' in popular diction stood for the (male or female) genital organ. S. W. Fores published a print by C. Williams with the title *A Representation of the Regent's Tremendous* Thing Erected *in the Park*.

of his time embroidering a silk petticoat for a statue of the Blessed Virgin), and for his brutal treatment of his liberal opponents. The Regent's yacht was the target for much objurgation as a source of great expense, and it was currently undergoing renovation.

A fresh humanitarian cause occupied Hone in 1816. This was in furtherance of a campaign initiated by Matthew Wood, whose activities as Lord Mayor included cleaning up some of the abuses of the City of London. The particular scandal which called forth Hone's exertions was the activity of a gang which enticed petty criminals to commit burglary, then a capital offence, inform on them, and when they were convicted claim the reward. One particular gang had been rounded up and was sentenced in September. This event called forth two tracts from Hone. One was the account of a shocking case in 1756, *Hone's Interesting History of the memorable Blood Conspiracy, carried on by S. MacDaniel* (and three others) *thief-takers, and their trials and sentences in 1756*. A frontispiece from a contemporary print of MacDaniel was engraved by George Cruikshank.

The London case was described in *Four Trials of the Blood Conspirators of 1816, The only authentic Report, with a Preface, etc.* In his *Catalogue* of *Books for Sale*, 1820, Hone describes this item, no. 994, as *Scarce*, and so prices it at 4s., a substantial sum for that day.

Alderman Wood was of course a butt of the Loyal faction, but greatly respected by the Radicals. His plan for clearing prostitutes from the streets was the subject of at least two ribald prints. Wood was to be ridiculed again for his championship of Queen Caroline.

V *The Three Trials of William Hone*

Already then, by the end of 1816, Hone's output had been flagrantly disrespectful to his social superiors. It is impossible that this should not have been taken note of in those quarters, but caricatures had hardly ever been successfully prosecuted. But now he took a step which enabled his opponents to lay their hands on him, albeit after some hesitation. His next and most dangerous move was to compose or concoct some parodies on parts of the Liturgy as published by authority in the Book of Common Prayer. These were five in number, each consisting of a half-sheet making, when folded, an eight-page tract. They were all priced at twopence, which aggravated the offence. The three prosecuted were *John Wilkes's Catechism*, *The Sinecurist's Creed* and *The Political Litany*; the other titles were *A Political Catechism, By an Englishman* and *The Bullet Te Deum; with The Canticle of the Stone*. When Hone withdrew the parodies, which he did in deference to his family's pietistic feelings, on 22 February Richard Carlile re-issued them. It is said that Hone made no objection but he could not in any case have prevented it. Carlile replaced Hone's imprint with a more aggressive one:

Printed and Published by R. Carlile, at the Republican Office, No. 183, Fleet Street, and sold by those who are not afraid of incurring the Displeasure of His Majesty's Ministers, their Spies or Informers, or Public Plunderers of any Denomination. 1817.

It is not known whether this had any effect on the Government's decision to proceed against Hone. Carlile was left alone in this instance, but he had more than enough coming to him.

It seems much more likely that it was Hone's next step which decided them to prosecute. The publisher of a radical weekly journal was well worth putting out of action. For Hone had now begun to edit and publish *The Reformists' Register*, a journal directed specifically against the Whigs and other plausible compromisers who were endeavouring to divert Reformists from the full rights of franchise. The following paragraph from a leaflet published after the first issue indicated the tone of the new journal: at the price of twopence and in the hands of skilful controversialists, any unpopular Government would have wished to get it out of the way.

No. I was published on Saturday, Feb. 1., 1817. The leading article of No. II for Feb. 8, 1817, is, UNIVERSAL SUFFRAGE and ANNUAL PARLIA-MENTS *against* Mr. BROUGHAM and the WHIGS. The leading article of No. III, for February 15, Sir F. BURDETT'S *Plan of Reform*, with other topics. No. IV, a Register Extraordinary, published on Monday, Feb. 17, against Mr. BROUGHAM's attacks on the Reformists. No. V, Feb. 22, Apostacy and Corruption.

It is clear that however distasteful such an expression of views might be to exalted politicians, it is improbable that any London jury would find them seditious. Hence the noisy denunciations in Parliament by Sidmouth and others of the liturgical parodies as an attack on the Christian religion.

A short quotation from *Wilkes's Catechism* will demonstrate the sort of fun that these 'little books' provided, poison to the sinecurist, but warmly to be appreciated in every walk of life where there was disgust at the corruption and inefficiency of the existing system. Here is a specimen:

A Catechism, that is to say, An Instruction, to be learned of every person before he be brought to be confirmed a Placeman or Pensioner by the Minister.
QUESTION: What is your name?
ANSWER: Lick Spittle
QUESTION: Who gave you this name?
ANSWER: My Sureties to the Ministry, in my Political Change, wherein I

was made a Member of the Majority, the Child of Corruption, and a Locust to devour the good things of this kingdom.

QUESTION: What did your sureties then for you?

ANSWER: They did promise and vow three things in my name. First, that I would renounce the Reformists and all their works, the pomps and vanity of Popular Favour, and all the sinful lusts of Independence. Secondly, that I should believe all the articles of the Court Faith. And thirdly, that I should keep the Minister's sole Will and Commandments, and walk in the same all the days of my life . . .

QUESTION: Rehearse the articles of thy belief.

ANSWER: I believe in George, the Regent Almighty, maker of New Streets, and Knights of the Bath.

And in the present Ministry, his only choice, who were conceived of Toryism, brought forth of William Pitt, suffered loss of Place under Charles James Fox, were execrated, dead and buried. In a few months they rose again from their minority: they reascended to the Treasury benches, and sit at the right hand of a little man with a large wig: from whence they laugh at the Petition of the People who may pray for Reform, and that the sweat of their brow may procure them bread.

The first issue of *The Yellow Dwarf*, A Weekly Miscellany launched by John Hunt on 3 January, 1818, a few days after Hone's acquittal carried on its front page an account and critical analysis of the proceedings against him—a matter on which the Proprietor of *The Examiner* was well qualified to comment. A point in its excellent summary is of particular application here.

Quoting Blackstone on proceeding by *ex-officio* informations instead of by indictment, their only proper use being 'For offences so high and dangerous, in the punishment or prevention of which, a moment's delay would be fatal', the paper goes on

Now it was stated in evidence and not disputed that the sale of the parodies had been discontinued long before the prosecution took place. The shopman of Hone's who gave evidence said that the Wilkes' Catechism had been on sale only about five days before it was stopped, on 22 February at the same time as that of the other parodies, which had been selling since the beginning of January. His reason for withdrawing the parodies, Hone said was that as soon as he was made aware of the publication having given offence to some persons whose opinion he respected, however much he might differ with them on that point, he immediately stopped the sale.

The Canticle of the Stone and *The Bullet Te Deum* derided the extravagant alarm whipped up about the incident in which a window of the Regent's coach was broken as he returned from the opening of Parliament on 28 January. So this last tract could not have been on sale till a day or two later than the others.

The first business of the new Parliament was to procure the suspension of Habeus Corpus. In the course of their justification for this, the Government produced a number of documents in a green bag and appointed Committees in each House to report on them. During the debates on the Bill, Sidmouth made much of the licentiousness of the Press, and Hone's tracts were specifically denounced as 'blasphemous' (though blasphemy was not charged in Court). *The Yellow Dwarf* commented:

The existence of 'blasphemous parodies' was made an article in the Bill of Indictment against the people of England on which the suspension of the Habeas Corpus Act was founded. They were held up as signs of the times quite as terrible as the projects of the Spenceans. . . . It is now for the public to decide whether they (the Government) were as foolish as they pretend to be, whether these prosecutions were instituted under the idea that these parodies *were* intended to bring Religion into contempt, or whether they originated in an enmity towards the author on political grounds. . . . We do not think it necessary to make strong asseverations to our own opinion on this subject, on which every man is well qualified to decide.

It cannot be too strongly pointed out that after Hone's voluntary suppression of the parodies (though this would do no more than mitigate the severity of the punishment if an offence had been proved), the Government made no move until 3 May, when Hone was taken into custody without any warning and remained confined for two months. He was then released on his own recognizances. It was assumed by Hone and others that after this infliction the proceedings against him would be dropped, as often happened with *ex officio* informations—they remained suspended as a kind of threat.

But Hone continued to give evidence of incorrigible malice, as it would seem to his opponents. Besides continuing the *Reformists' Register*, in spite of the rumours of impending action against him, he issued a squib lampooning Lord Eldon's domestic parsimony. After incarceration in the King's Bench for two months owing to his inability to find bail (two sureties of a thousand pounds on *each* of the misdemeanours charged against him), he put out two little pieces ridiculing Castlereagh, who had been reported bitten by a dog. (See *Black Dwarf*, 6 August 1817, under the heading 'Shocking Occurrence'. Here the Editor, Wooler, suggested applying a mixture of salt and gunpowder to the wound, as had been found effective in Ireland after floggings.) In September Hone was guying Sidmouth for the panic measures he had taken to deal with the Bartholomew Fair Insurrection, which a hoaxer had announced would break out during that month. All these little pieces carried suitably grotesque designs by George Cruikshank.

The Government must have reckoned that Hone would not be able to put up much of a defence against the leading law officer of the Crown, supported by a judge whose loyalty had already dictated to him what verdict he should strive to have recorded. Not that there was any expectation of it taking very long. The man was not represented by

Counsel, and it was easy to embarrass a lone defendant with a point of law. Anyway, Hone seemed so obviously guilty.

Certainly no lawyer could have got Hone off clear, for lawyers think legalistically, like judges. Hone addressed himself entirely to the jury and juries think in human terms, if they are allowed to.

A verbatim, or very full, report of each trial was on sale very shortly after the verdict had been given. To try a man three times for what was virtually the same offence was almost unprecedented and the result was awaited through the country with the intensest interest. The discomfiture of the Prosecution and the judges was a thing to tickle the heart of an ordinary human being, who knows instinctively that much profanity is inseparable from human experience, and not to be eradicated by solemn sinners in long wigs.

Hone asserts that he never recovered from the strain of his long anticipation of imprisonment with its effect on his uncertain health and certain penury for his large family. He had already suffered one stroke and was later to become partially paralysed. It is indeed remarkable that he could bear up to the three days' ordeal—and in fact, he declared in court that the Government was determined to defeat him if necessary through his sheer physical exhaustion. He had spoken altogether for twenty-one hours in three days, amidst many attendant handicaps—the Court was at Guildhall, and crowded to suffocation all the time. At the days' end he was too weary to take proper nourishment. It is surprising that Hone's has never been included in any series of famous trials—the subject seems to me more interesting than murder, and there is a lot of fun to be had from the exchanges between prisoner and judge or Attorney-General.

Hone was a free man again, and the most popular man in Britain. He was also penniless. Fortunately, many of those who had helped him in one way or another during the preparation of his defence knew of his situation, and a few days after his acquittal an important dinner at the City of London Tavern was organised by the Friends of Trial by Jury and Liberty of the Press. Amongst its objects was the launching of a Subscription 'for the purpose of enabling WILLIAM HONE to surmount the difficulties in which he has been placed by being selected by the Ministers of the Crown as the object of their persecution'. Alderman Waithman was in the Chair, and the very numerous assembly ('amongst whom we observed several elegantly dressed females' the reporter noted) was addressed by Sir Francis Burdett, James Perry (Editor of the *Morning Chronicle*), Lord Cochrane, and T. J. Wooler, the daring Editor of *The Black Dwarf*, who had been imprisoned before trial at the same time as Hone. Also among the speakers, and included in the votes of thanks, was Charles Pearson, a lawyer whose services, freely rendered to both Wooler and Hone, were responsible for the fact that the juries at their trials were not 'packed', as was usual in political trials, but 'pricked', that is, taken haphazard from a complete list of eligible jurymen.

Appended to the printed report of the Meeting is a list of Contributors which includes in the first edition some six hundred names, 'those so far received'. Even a cursory glance down the columns reveals that the strength of feeling about the relevance of the trial extended far beyond the metropolis, that it was nation-wide and included many who would have been very far from thinking of themselves as radicals. The social historian will find some rich 'atmospheric' colouring of the contemporary scene in this straightforward record of plain men's uninhibited relief.

	£	
His Grace the Duke of Bedford	105	
The Marquis of Tavistock	50	
The Earl of Darlington	105	
The Earl of Sefton	105	
A Member of the House of Lords—an enemy to persecution, and especially to religious persecution, employed for political purposes	100	
Sir Francis Burdett, Bart.	100	
Lord Cochrane	100	
25 one, and 5 five pound notes, from a Lady unknown	50	
A Country Gentleman	2	
Francis Canning, Foxcote, near Shipston-on-Stour	10	
Joshua Grigsby, Drinkston, Suffolk	10	
Rev. F. Treleaven, Reading	1	
William Hallett, Berks.	5	5s
Godfrey Higgins, Skellow-grange, Yorkshire	5	
Wm. Lawrence, M.D., College of Physicians	5	
Seven Friends at Liverpool	30	
J. T. Mount, St. Albans, Caerleon	1	
T. Groom, late Mayor of Maidenhead	1	

Individual subscriptions which have a particular interest include the following:

A Musselman, who thinks it would not be an impious libel to parody the Koran	1	
Sir Richard Phillips	5	5s
Percy B. Shelley, Marlow	5	
William Frend	5	5s
May the Unblemished Hone never want the Oil of Justice	1	
Captain Milligans Spilligans Hilligans, of the Ship Reform, bound for Toleration Port	1	
Thomas Creevy, M.P.	10	
Enemies to Jeffries, from Fifeshire	5	
A swarm of B's from Somersetshire, whose stings are for the oppressors of Law, and whose honey is for the oppressed by Law	5	

There were several ghosts on the List:

The ghosts of Jeffries and Sir William Noy
The ghost of Horne Tooke
The ghost of Dr. Slop's Dirty Shirt
The ghost of Judge Jefferies
The spirit of Sir William Jones
The ghosts of Ludlam and Turner by Mrs. Blake
  [These two had been hanged after the Pentridge Rising]

Dr. Samuel Parr sent a pound to the fund:

From Samuel Parr, D.D. who most seriously disapproves of all Parodies upon the hallowed language of Scripture, and the contents of the Prayer Book, but acquits Mr. Hone of intentional impiety, admires his talents and his fortitude, and applauds the good sense and integrity of his juries.

I also include here some comments on Hone and his acquittal, from literary circles:

Hone the publisher's trial you must find very amusing; and as Englishmen very encouraging—his *Not Guilty* is a thing, which not to have been, would have dulled still more Liberty's Emblazoning—Lord Ellenborough has been paid in his own coin—Wooler and Hone have done us an essential service.

> *Keats, to his brothers George and Thomas, 22 December 1817*

Percy B. Shelley, Marlow, to the Subscription for Hone, 1817. £5

I was glad to see Coleridge take the right side on Hone's trial. He eloquently expatiated on the necessity of saving Hone in order to save English law, and he derided the legal definition of a libel, whatever tends to produce certain consequences—without any regard to the intention of the publisher.

> *H. C. Robinson, at Charles Lamb's, 27 December 1817*

The acquittal of Hone is enough to make one out of love with English Juries.

> *Wordsworth to T. Monkhouse, January 1818*

He had moved from his small shop in the Old Bailey to a large and expensive house on Ludgate Hill. Here he was followed, caressed and praised by a succession of visitors—real, or affected friends,—amongst whom were some of the most popular members of opposition in the two Houses. . . . I knew him well and respected him for warmth of heart, kindness of disposition, and strength of head; but he was most improvident and indiscreet in the management of money affairs.

> *John Britton, Auto-Biography.*

Nor do I owe to these alone
My great success; but much to HONE
The parodist, who was acquitted,
And who the *Judge himself* out-witted.
The first day ABB-T tried the case,
Whilst E--NB--H's learned face
(As chancery bill, almost as long)
Perceiv'd *state matters* going wrong;
And, arm'd with all his power—HE
(Of vengeance the *fac simile*)
Wou'd hear the second day, and last,
As who shou'd say "he *shall* be cast:"
HONE pleaded for himself—his story,
So clear, and with *a fortiori*,
That, *ergo*, all his Jurys pitied him;
They saw him *guiltless*, and *acquitted* him.
This great defeat his Lordship gall'd,
In short it all the Bar appall'd:
Nor was it likely to do less;—
Their OBJECT was against the PRESS.

> *Thomas Brown* [that is, Thomas Moore]
> '*Replies to the Letters of The Fudge Family in Paris*', 1818

VI *A Mirage of Affluence*

The subscription fund totalled over three thousand pounds, but Hone complains that he received far less than this, owing to the expenses of advertising and inefficiency. But he moved from his cramped quarters in Old Bailey to a fairly large house at 45 Ludgate Hill, and for a few years lived a life of some comfort and tranquillity. He was disillusioned with bookselling, and regretted that some of his friends had invested his money in a stock of books. 'People came in and looked at a set of Johnson or Shakespeare, and went out with a shilling pamphlet', he told a neighbour in later life. But he increased his activity in 'making' books, often, he confesses, by cutting up others:

One day, walking down Holborn, I stopped at an old book stall; there I found a book open with some stories in it that I saw at once would throw some light upon some of my old prints that I could learn nothing about. The book was Jeremiah Jones on the Canon of Scripture; the stories were the Apochryphal Gospels. When I had studied my prints with them, and found what light they threw on their subjects, I thought they would do for the public, particularly for antiquarians and print collectors; so I took a pair of scissors (for that is the way I make books) and cut out what I wanted, and sent them to the printers, and out came my Apocryphal Gospels that made such a noise in the world.

It will be seen from the advertisements included in the pamphlets, that Hone did in this phase of his career put together a very interesting, idiosyncratic list of publications. His intention had been, as he states in the Preface to his Trials, to become a 'respectable' publisher, by which I suppose he means one publishing substantial volumes, not merely pamphlets. Though he announces several impressions of some, the financial result seems to have been not wholly satisfactory.

To this period of Hone's activities we owe the publication of Hazlitt's collected *Political Essays*. Certainly no other publisher would have been willing at that time to invest money in printing such a large volume of such an uncompromisingly oppositional character. I do not think any one of Hazlitt's biographers has been generous enough in recognising the courage of Hone's action, for the book runs to over four hundred pages, and he paid the author a hundred pounds into the bargain. It does not seem to have done the publisher much good, for we find the sheets bound up with a cancel-title under the imprint of Simpkin Marshall in only three years time.

Another 'scissors' job was issued under a pseudonym, but its contents reveal a number of Hone's preoccupations:

Sixty Curious and Authentic Narratives and Anecdotes respecting Extraordinary Characters: illustrative of the tendency of credulity and fanaticism; exemplifying the imperfections of circumstantial evidence; and recording singular instances of voluntary human suffering, and interesting occurrences. By John Cecil Esq.

This work is listed under Hone's entry in the BM Catalogue as pseudonymous. But another work published by Hone in the same year, *The Age of Intellect*, with a frontispiece by Cruikshank (drawn by the ostensible author Francis Moore) is entered only under Moore. I say ostensible author advisedly, for it is no other than the famous seer and almanack-maker, whose death is given as ?1715 in the *Dictionary of National Biography*. The query need not bother us, as it is not intended to suggest his return to authorship in 1819. This Moore is not credited with any other publications, and it is suggestive that the subjects treated in this facetious hodge-podge are such as we know to have been of interest to Hone and were currently discussed around 1819, such as the visit of the 'Circassian Beauty' in the Persian Ambassador's suite. The attribution to Hone is further made plausible by his admiring reference to Keats, Hazlitt and others in the Liberal ambiance. (Hone made several references to Keats in his *Every Day Book* and quoted him at length—perhaps the earliest to do so.)

The matter of authorship was clinched for me by the whimsical prefatorial addresses to Bob Blazon. Bob Blazon, of course, was a creation of Tom Brown the Younger, alias Thomas Moore, one of the correspondents in his epistolary sequences with the Fudge Family.

Now at the end of 1818 Moore published *Replies to the Letters of the Fudge Family in Paris* (quoted from on page 21) which included two pieces celebrating Hone's acquittal. And who is more likely to have been interested in this and to have wished to convey an acknowledgement to the writer than the victim of the case himself?

VII   *The Pamphlet War*

It is given to very few to become a national figure on two separate counts, but it very definitely was so with Hone. His second apotheosis is not prefigured in anything produced during the two years 1818 and 1819 till the last month of the latter, almost exactly two years after his acquittal. And there is no doubt that there would have been no such furore had the *Political House that Jack Built* been issued without the illustrations of George Cruikshank.

For the greater part of these two years Hone had been fully occupied with the preparation of his 'respectable' publications, and with the accumulation of material for the 'History of Parody' which he had promised to compile in the Preface to the collected version of his trials issued early in January 1818. It was on his definition of parody and its relation to the original parodied that his defence had turned, and on which he established his defence more generally. The fate of this history of parody is another of the minor tragedies which afflicted Hone owing to the complete lack of method in his handling of his financial affairs. During his brief spell of affluence he says. 'As long as the money lasted, I used to go to my cashier for £5 or £10 at a time, generally to buy old prints and curious books; at last, asking for money, he said there were no funds. I insisted; "I *must* have the books I have been looking at"—he gave me the last'.

Finally, the fine collection he had amassed was put in pledge for a loan, and when not redeemed it was sold *en bloc* for a fraction of its value. The last announcement of the imminent publication of the 'History of Parody' was in 1824.

Whilst engaged with a new type of publishing Hone had not found much occasion for the employment of Cruikshank's talents. A couple of frontispieces and some reduced copies of earlier caricatures to illustrate the 'History of Parody' are all that have been traced. But there is no doubt that the two men remained friends, for as soon as he had roughed-out the text of his nursery rhyme made applicable to present circumstances, he found Cruikshank to hand and readily agreeable to co-operate. Mrs. Rolleston fortunately preserved Hone's recollection of the origin of his most famous production:

'After my trial, the newspapers were continually at me, calling me an acquitted felon. The worm will turn when trodden on. One day, when I had been exasperated beyond bearing, one of my children, a little girl of four years old, was sitting on my knee, very busy looking at the pictures of a child's book. "What have you got there?" said I;—"the house that Dack built"—an idea flashed across my mind; I saw at once the use that might be made of it; I took it away from her. I said—"Mother, take the child, send me up my tea and two candles, and let nobody come near me till I ring." I sat up all night and wrote—'The house that Jack built.' In the morning, I sent for Cruikshank, read it to him, and put myself into the attitudes of the figures I wanted drawn. Some of the characters Cruikshank had never seen; but I gave him the likeness as well as the attitude;' and so saying, he at once put himself into the character of Lord Lyndhurst—there introduced as a wigged rat; Cruikshank had never seen him; but the character had a most whimsical resemblance.

But besides the rankling of an old grievance, there must have been a more immediate irritation to goad him into an abrupt return to the satire of the contemporary political scene, which he had apparently let pass him by for almost two years since the last small squibs preceding his trial. The year had been one of mounting tension, which seemed to have reached a climax with the Peterloo assault in August. Contemporaneously, Shelley was impelled to express the intolerable sense of degradation which burdened the atmosphere:

> An old, mad, blind, despised, and dying king,—
> Princes, the dregs of their dull race, who flow
> Through public scorn—mud from a muddy spring,—
> Rulers, who neither see, nor feel, nor know,
> But leech-like to their fainting country cling . . .
> A people starved and stabbed in the untilled field.
>
> From *England in 1819*

Shelley's sonnet was not published at the time. It would in any case have had a hardly perceptible effect on public opinion. Hone's nursery rhyme had the merit, as propaganda, of slipping under the reader's guard, so that he found himself laughing and accepting a point against his rulers at which the conscious mind might have jibbed. Most readers would be grateful for having had a good laugh, without realising that their political innocence had been shattered for ever. In the later squibs the intention is clear, the wit is keener, but its edge is uncompromisingly lethal. Published in December, by March *The Political House that Jack Built* was in its fifty-second edition, and a *de-luxe* edition on drawing paper was on sale at three shillings, coloured.

At this point I would like to quote a few extracts from contemporary writers, in comparison with which Hone appears not at all extravagant in his censure of the dominant politicians:

The intensity of feeling, shown towards the crooked course of Castlereagh and his compeers, can hardly be judged aright by those who are not old enough to remember their unrelenting efforts to crush the liberties of the people, under the corrupt regency and selfish reign of George IV.

THOMAS COOPER, the Chartist. Address to the Reader,
Poetical Works, 1877

When Lord Castlereagh paid the debt to Nature, in August, 1822, the state indeed and its functionaries did honour to his memory. His remains were buried in Westminster Abbey. Great personages walked in procession, holding the pall; but the people shouted at the porch. A witness of that terrible manifestation of popular feeling, I can answer there was no expression of sorrow or respect in that shout.

R. R. MADDEN, *The United Irishmen*, 2nd edition, 1860

To Wellington
You are 'the best of cut-throats', do not start—
  The phrase is Shakespeare's, and not misapplied:—
War's a brain-spattering, windpipe-slitting art,
  Unless her cause by right be sanctified.
If you have acted *once* a generous part,
  The world, not the world's master, will decide,
And I shall be delighted to learn who,
Save you and yours, have gained by Waterloo?
BYRON, *Don Juan*, Canto Nine

One of the most generally detested practices of the administration was the employment of *agents provocateurs*. The following lines, coming from one so naturally non-partisan as Lamb, authenticate the satirical violence of more politically-minded men.

THE THREE GRAVES
These lines were written during the time of the spy system

Close by the ever-burning brimstone beds,
Where Bedlow, Oates, and Judas hide their heads,
I saw great Satan like a Sexton stand,
With his intolerable spade in hand,
Digging three graves. Of coffin shape they were
For those who coffinless must enter there,
With unblest rites. The shrouds were of that cloth
Which Clotho weaveth in her blackest wrath.
The dismal tinct oppressed the eye, which dwelt
Upon it long, like darkness to be felt.
The pillows to these baleful beds were toads,
Large, living, livid, melancholy loads,
Whose softness shocked. Worms of all monstrous size
Crawled round; and one, upcoiled, that never coils.
A dismal bell, inculcating despair,
Was always ringing in the heavy air:

And all about the detestable pit
Strange headless ghosts, and quarter'd forms did flit;
Rivers of blood from dripping traitors spilt,
By treachery stung from poverty to guilt.
I asked the Fiend, for whom those rites were meant?
'These graves', quoth he, 'when life's short oil is spent,—
When the dark night comes, and they're sinking bedwards—
I mean for Castles, Oliver and Edwards'.

CHARLES LAMB, from a MS reproduced in
Sidelights on Charles Lamb by Bertram
Dobell, 1903

The immense success of *The Political House* needed to be followed up
without delay, to be capitalised. For once, Hone did not allow himself to be distracted by any of his many, worthy enthusiasms. The
second tract, *The Man in the Moon*, was published early in January
1820. Its success almost rivalled that of the first, and by March it was
in its 26th edition. Once again, topicality had been the driving force.
For whilst the then recent horror of Peterloo had been the dominant
theme of the first, its successor was a light-hearted take-off of the
threatening speech by the Regent at the new session of Parliament
on November 23rd.

It was common knowledge that when Parliament reassembled the
Cabinet meant to ask for sterner measures of repression and re-
prisal against any expression of the extreme indignation that was
sweeping the country. Cruikshank's woodcuts in *The Man in the
Moon* are very light, and full of movement, whilst those of the *House*
had been (emotionally) static. It is not indignation that is dominant
now, but contempt at the Government's disingenuous antics in
pursuit of their transparently obnoxious ends.

The new legislation designed to tranquillise the restless populace
was the famous Six Acts, the Gagging Bills, introduced, debated and
receiving the Royal Assent in exactly one month. In spite of the
spirited way in which Cruikshank responded, two of these Six Acts,
those which disciplined the Press, were for a time successful, severely
handicapping the circulation of cheap periodicals or anything priced
at less than sixpence.

On the last leaf of *The Man in the Moon* Hone asserts that in view
of the numerous satires claiming to be written *By the Author of the
Political House that Jack Built*, he must insist that none is genuinely
the work of that author unless published by Hone himself. 'And that
his last, and owing to imperative claims upon his pen of a higher order,
possibly his very last production in that way, will be found in THE
MAN IN THE MOON.'

The 'claims of a higher order' must refer to the *History of Parody*,
promised at the conclusion of his three trials. He had been gathering

material for it, old books and prints, ever since, to the point of insolvency. But the intention, obviously sincerely felt, was not to be sustained. An event took place, not unforseen, but of unpredictable consequences, which called for the exercise of his satiric talents in defence of a maligned female and his lawful Queen. Had it been left to his choice, he would not have involved himself in the action. Caroline, now that George III was deceased and her husband on the throne, returned to England in the expectation of being, or at least in the determination to insist on being, crowned Queen of England beside her husband at his coronation.

The new king's horror at this prospect was widely known. Caroline's conduct whilst residing abroad had been undoubtedly flamboyant, certainly indiscreet, possibly adulterous. The king's desire to marry again and perhaps get an heir to the throne was reasonable enough. That his own conduct had been delinquent is beside the point. Justice would not be served by forcing him to cohabit with a detested woman. But the matter became a party issue, as indeed it had become years before, when the Whigs played off the Princess of Wales and her daughter Charlotte against the Prince, who had taken refuge behind a High Tory Administration.

Now, after Princess Charlotte's early death the Whigs, or a faction of them, rallied round the Queen, so that when a Bill of Pains and Penalties was issued against her, her innocence became inextricably entangled with Parliamentary reform and the Radical programme.

Hone found himself in a dilemma when he was approached by leaders of the Reform movement, to assist her cause. Here is his own account, as related to his neighbour Mrs. Rolleston, shortly before his death. The Queen landed in England on 5 June 1820, but her return had been confidently expected some time before that.

I wanted to write a history of parody. I was reading in the British Museum for that purpose—that was at the time of the Queen's business, some of her chief partisans came to me. They urged me to write something for her. I refused for some time, till at last they said, 'The Queen expects it of you', and I felt I could no longer refuse; but it troubled me very much. I had gone there to be quiet, and out of the way of politics, about which my mind had begun to misgive me; that is, as to my interference with them. Observe, though God has changed my opinions about religion, I have not changed my politics. I did not like my task; I could not see how to do it, nor yet how to avoid it; so a good deal out of sorts, I left the Museum. Instead of going straight home, I wandered off towards Pentonville, and stopped and looked absently into the window of a little fancy shop—there was a toy, 'The matrimonial ladder.' I saw at once what I could do with that, and went home and wrote 'The Queen's Matrimonial Ladder.' Soon after, a person, whom I shall not name, came and offered me £50 to suppress it. I refused. I was offered up to £500. I said, 'Could you not make it £5,000? If you did, I should refuse it.'

The Bill of Pains and Penalties against the Queen was introduced into the House of Lords by Lord Liverpool, Prime Minister, on 17 August. The pamphlet was probably issued shortly before. It sold rapidly, as it was so superbly topical. Also there is more 'story' in it than in the earlier satires. Priced at one shilling, including the 'toy', it was a bargain. Bias apart, it is a good summary of the sad story of a marriage for dynastic convenience. The Princess is represented with a tender dignity not overdone, and the Prince's character, though savagely exposed, meets with such fantastic retribution that the cruelty is scarcely felt. 'Cat's meat!' is an intolerable finale.

Hone continued to support the Queen both by satire of her opponents and some rather sentimental effusions of his own. '*Non mi Ricordo*' is based on the extravagant behaviour of one of the Italian witnesses brought over to give evidence, whose repeated 'I don't remember' when pressed to substantiate specific details, produced hilarity throughout the country and beyond. The expression even slips incongruously into a pamphlet Byron was writing, in Italy. All the same, Majocchi's obvious mendacity did not much benefit the Queen's case.

In *The Political Showman—at Home* the inventiveness of author and artist is most copious. It is the best of the pamphlets, taken as a whole, I think, though there are cuts in other pamphlets more intensely imaginative (I think particularly of the title-page and final cut of *The Right Divine of Kings to Govern Wrong*, p. 303–4).

The *Political Showman* is a synthetic exposure of all the evil incorporated in the functions of an autocratic system of Government. Although it pillories individuals it is, of course, aiming at the principle. Britain was not yet in the condition delineated, but there were real fears of its declining into such ignominy—hence the almost sentimental reverence evoked by the slogans 'Trial by Jury' and 'Liberty of the Press'. Our government was friends with all the reactionary thrones of Europe, and by its policy over twenty years had ensured that there were no others. It was a time at which not to feel threatened was to be blind to realities.

The genial relationship of Hone and Cruikshank in their collaboration is well shown in a mock-scolding letter from the former, which is quoted by Cohn in his classic work on Cruikshank. In 1821 Hone complains that he cannot get on with his publications

... without my friend Cruikshank will forswear late hours, blue ruin and dollies—all which united, are unfriendly to certain mechanical motions of the spirit, which I tell George would make him a trustworthy 'man of business', whereunto, he hath of late answered to the purport or effect following: 'You be d—d', or 'Go to Hell', or else when he hath been less under the influence of 'daffy', he has invited me in rather a dictatorial tone to 'Go and teach my Granny to suck eggs!' This demoniac possession is on him even now, for he came yesterday afternoon, to insist that I should forthwith proceed to the worthy Alderman Waithman, and get the watchhouse keeper of an adjoining parish dismissed for having differed with him in opinion upon a point a few evenings ago—not choosing to do this, he sent for a pipe, and blew clouds of tobacco smoke over me and my books, in my hall of Parody, for a couple of hours, demanded entrance to my wife's bedroom to shave and smarten himself for an evening party, took possession of my best 'Brandenburg' pumps, damned me under the denomination of 'Old Robin Gray', because I had not a *chapeau bras*, otherwise discomposed the wonted order of my mind and household and manifested what I have long suspected, that he is by no means friendly to Reform! (Quoted in A. Cohn, *George Cruikshank* 1924)

1820 was a vintage year for author, artist and publisher, seeing the original appearance of four items, one a revival, the other three amongst the most brilliant of the satires they concocted together: *The Right Divine of Kings to Govern Wrong, The Spirit of Despotism, The Political Showman—at Home*, and *A Slap at Slop*. The first, third and fourth include some of Cruikshank's finest inventions, so Hone's remonstrance served a good purpose.

To have included the last and longest of the squibs would have unduly lengthened this book, and there was no riposte at all—all the intellectual resources of the Bridge Street Gang were inadequate to concoct one. *A Slap at Slop and the Bridge Street Gang* shows no slackening in wit or vitality of design. But its target is a particular bunch of individuals of little general interest. The activities of the Constitutional Association were ostensibly to be devoted to countering the publications of Radicals and Reformers against which the Attorney-General was too supine to proceed. This they did unsuccessfully and the pamphlet suggests that the subscriptions were allocated to private ends.

The *Slap at Slop* was originally issued in newspaper format, and this layout gave the needed prominence to Hone's parodies of journalistic features and pseudo-advertisements with brilliant Cruikshankian ideograms. Three very large blocks, across three columns, are most memorable. A smaller design, the Peterloo Medal, has become widely known. The newspaper had to be laid out fresh when folded to octavo format for inclusion in the collective volume; this causes some loss of the vigour it has on a full sheet, but it is no less a brilliant farewell to their last collaboration in this field.

A very famous plate etched by Cruikshank for a serious hoax which he and Hone contrived in common (for in spite of George Cruikshank's many fallacious claims to be the originator of the text as well as the designs of the works he illustrated, it is plausible to allow him a large share in this project), *The Bank Restriction Barometer* consisted of an envelope containing a fantasised bank note, in which the main feature is a line of men and women hanging from the gallows. The frequent executions for passing forged one-pound notes which the Bank's representative often had difficulty in asserting to be forgeries, had become a scandal. The Note was a brilliant stroke in the campaign to alter the law, in which many others had a hand.

The *Slap at Slop* was incontestably the last of Hone's squibs, though bibliographers sometimes claim later ones as his. He published the last book under his own imprint in 1823 and his last pamphlet, a defence against attacks on his *Apochryphal New Testament*, in 1824.

The book, *Ancient Mysteries Described*, is remarkable as a pioneer effort to introduce the literary and dramatic merits of the late medieval play-cycles to popular appreciation. His inclusion of the Cherry Tree Carol indicates his true sense of poetry. One remembers a passage in his first Trial, when he quotes the lyric beginning 'The first great joy that Mary had', to the acute distress of the Attorney General's modesty. Hone was naturally free of the false good taste which was for long the bane of the literary establishment. He was far better equipped than any university don would have been to foster the understanding and enjoyment of our older literature and the traditions on which it drew. It was the basis of his success in his last long and arduous task.

The rest of the year 1824 must have been fully employed in seeking out material, both literary and illustrative, for the *Every Day Book*, which was announced to appear each week in threepenny parts of sixteen pages—a promise faithfully carried out after some preliminary irregularity, which was cured by a friendly admonition from Charles Lamb.

But hardly had the first year's volume of the *Every Day Book* been completed than his financial vulnerability brought him to a desperate situation. He was imprisoned for debt in 1826, as we learn from a letter of his to Rev. W. J. Fox, lecturer at South Place Chapel: '3 June . . . I have come under the extreme power of the law, by the inforcement of just claims upon me which I am unable to discharge. . . . I have been separated from my family for six weeks, during which time they were homeless. We have got together again at last in a little house by ourselves.'

To extricate himself he had to pledge the valuable collection of books and prints which he had accumulated to write his *History of Parody*; he never regained possession of it. He finished the *Every Day Book* in 1826 and compiled an equally entertaining volume, called the *Table Book* in 1827. These three volumes totalled over 2000 pages, with 436 illustrations. He was then obliged to transfer his property in them to Thomas Tegg, a more successful publisher, for whom he compiled a similar volume, *The Year Book*, in 1831.

In 1830 Charles Lamb had been instrumental in getting *The Times* to open a Subscription Fund for Hone, to enable him to become proprietor of The Grasshopper Coffee House and Reading Room in Gracechurch Street. The appeal was successful but the enterprise was not.

From then on, the record tells of declining activity, the effect of bad health and increasing religious preoccupations. In 1834, Hone and some of his family were received into one of the Congregational churches in London. He used sometimes to preach at the Weigh-house Chapel, Eastcheap.

He later moved out to Tottenham, but had to visit the city regularly as he had been appointed editor of a Dissenting journal, The Patriot, at £2 a week. His health deteriorated and he became partially paralysed. H. C. Robinson has an entry in his Diary, 17 February, 1841 'I went to Joe Parke's [lawyer, active Reformer] in search of him, meaning to give £5 to him for poor Hone, for whom he wrote a begging letter.'

George Cruikshank visited Hone in his decline and regretted that he had allowed their old friendship to lapse in recent years. He died late in 1842 and the following February *The Gentleman's Magazine* carried a respectful obituary which concludes:

'In society, Mr. Hone was a cheerful companion, and his heart was never closed against the complaints of his fellow-creatures. Out of a family of twelve children, nine are still living, several of whom, with their widowed mother, we regret to say, are left almost wholly un-provided for.'

Somehow, the future made amends, for we hear of his widow surviving 'a fine, intelligent old lady' at the age of 82. And two of his daughters were proprietors of a school for many years after that.

There is no doubt that Hone would prefer to be remembered for his anthologies rather than his satires and Charles Lamb paid them a fitting tribute in the verses he inscribed to 'the parodist':

TO THE EDITOR OF THE 'EVERY DAY BOOK'

I like you, and your book, ingenious Hone!
    In whose capacious all-embracing leaves
The very marrow of tradition's shown;
    And all that history—much that fiction—weaves.

By every sort of taste your work is graced;
    Vast stores of modern anecdote we find,
With good old story quaintly interlaced—
    The theme as various as the reader's mind . . .

Rags, relics, witches, ghosts, fiends, crown your page;
  Our fathers' mummeries we well-pleased behold,
And, proudly conscious of a purer age,
  Forgive some fopperies in the times of old . . .

Dan Phoebus loves your book,—trust me, friend Hone—
  The title only errs, he bids me say:
For while such art, wit, reading, there are shown,
  He swears, 'tis not a work of *every day*.

THE PAMPHLETS

THE POLITICAL

HOUSE

THAT

JACK BUILT.

" A straw—thrown up to show which way the wind blows."

WITH THIRTEEN CUTS.

The Pen and the Sword.

Thirtieth Edition.

LONDON:
PRINTED BY AND FOR WILLIAM HONE, LUDGATE HILL.

1819.

ONE SHILLING.

—— " Many, whose sequester'd lot
Forbids their interference, looking on,
Anticipate perforce some dire event ;
And, seeing the old castle of the state,
That promis'd once more firmness, so assail'd,
That all its tempest-beaten turrets shake,
Stand motionless expectants of its fall."

Cowper.

NOTE.

Each Motto that follows, is from Cowper's " Task."

THE AUTHOR'S

DEDICATION

TO HIS POLITICAL GODCHILD.

TO

DOCTOR SLOP,

IN ACKNOWLEDGMENT OF

MANY PUBLIC TESTIMONIALS OF HIS FILIAL GRATITUDE;

AND TO

THE NURSERY OF CHILDREN,

SIX FEET HIGH,

HIS READERS,

FOR THE DELIGHT AND INSTRUCTION OF

THEIR UNINFORMED MINDS;

THIS JUVENILE PUBLICATION

IS AFFECTIONATELY INSCRIBED,

BY

THE DOCTOR'S POLITICAL GODFATHER,

THE AUTHOR.

NOTE.—*The Publication wherein the Author of " The Political House that Jack Built" conferred upon Dr. SLOP the lasting distinction of his name, was a Jeu d'Esprit, entitled " Buonaparte-phobia, or Cursing made easy to the meanest capacity,"—it is reprinted, and may be had of the Publisher, Price One Shilling.*

"A distant age asks where the fabric stood."

THIS IS THE HOUSE THAT JACK BUILT.

—— " Not to understand a treasure's worth,
Till time has stolen away the slighted good,
Is cause of half the poverty we feel,
And makes the world the wilderness it is."

THIS IS

THE WEALTH

that lay

In the House that Jack built.

B

——————— " A race obscene,
Spawn'd in the muddy beds of Nile, came forth,
Polluting Egypt : gardens, fields, and plains,
Were cover'd with the pest ;
The croaking nuisance lurk'd in every nook ;
Nor palaces, nor even chambers, 'scap'd ;
And the land stank—so num'rous was the fry.

———————

THESE ARE

THE VERMIN

That Plunder the Wealth,
That lay in the House,
That Jack built.

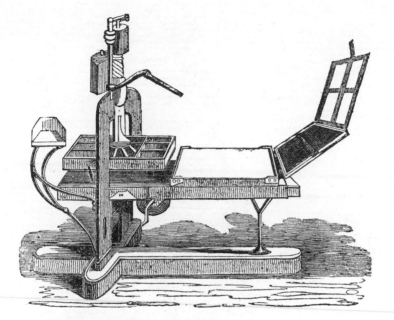

" Once enslaved, farewell!

*　　*　　*　　*

Do I forebode impossible events,
And tremble at vain dreams ? Heav'n grant I may !"

THIS IS

THE THING,

that, in spite of new Acts,

And attempts to restrain it,

by Soldiers or Tax,

Will *poison* the Vermin,

That plunder the Wealth,

That lay in the House,

That Jack built.

" The seals of office glitter in his eyes ;
He climbs, he pants, he grasps them—
To be a pest where he was useful once."

THIS IS

THE PUBLIC INFORMER,

who

Would put down the *Thing*,

that, in spite of new Acts,

And attempts to restrain it,

by Soldiers or Tax,

Will *poison* the Vermin, that plunder the Wealth,

That lay in the House, that Jack built.

"Ruffians are abroad——

*   *   *   *

Leviathan is not *so* tamed."

THESE ARE

THE *REASONS* OF LAWLESS POWER

That back the Public Informer,

who

Would put down the *Thing*,

that, in spite of new Acts,

And attempts to restrain it,

by Soldiers or Tax,

Will *poison* the Vermin,

That plunder the Wealth,

That lay in the House,

That Jack built.

——————— " Great offices will have
Great talents."

This is THE MAN—all shaven and shorn,
All cover'd with Orders—and all forlorn ;

THE DANDY OF SIXTY,

who bows with a grace,
And has *taste* in wigs, collars,
cuirasses and lace ;
Who, to tricksters, and fools,
leaves the State and its treasure,
And, when Britain's in tears,
sails about at his pleasure:
Who spurn'd from his presence
the Friends of his youth,
And now has not one
who will tell him the truth ;
Who took to his counsels,
in evil hour,
The Friends to the Reasons
of lawless Power ;
That back the Public Informer,
who
Would put down the *Thing*,
that, in spite of new Acts,
And attempts to restrain it,
by Soldiers or Tax,
Will *poison* the Vermin,
That plunder the Wealth,
That lay in the House,
That Jack built.

" Portentous, unexampled, unexplain'd !
——————————— What man seeing this,
And having human feelings, does not blush,
And hang his head, to think himself a man ?
————————————— I cannot rest
A silent witness of the headlong rage,
Or heedless folly, by which thousands die——
Bleed gold for Ministers to sport away."

THESE ARE

THE PEOPLE

all tatter'd and torn,

Who curse the day

wherein they were born,

On account of Taxation

too great to be borne,

And pray for relief,

from night to morn ;

Who, in vain, Petition

in every form,

Who, peaceably Meeting
        to ask for Reform,
Were sabred by Yeomanry Cavalry,
        who,
Were thank'd by THE MAN,
        all shaven and shorn,
All cover'd with Orders—
        and all forlorn ;
THE DANDY OF SIXTY,
        who bows with a grace,
And has *taste* in wigs, collars,
        cuirasses, and lace ;
Who, to tricksters, and fools,
        leaves the State and its treasure,
And when Britain's in tears,
        sails about at his pleasure ;
Who spurn'd from his presence
        the Friends of his youth,
And now has not one
        who will tell him the truth ;
Who took to his counsels, in evil hour,
The Friends to the Reasons of lawless Power,
That back the Public Informer, who
Would put down the *Thing*, that, in spite of new Acts,
And attempts to restrain it, by Soldiers or Tax,
Will *poison* the Vermin, that plunder the Wealth,
That lay in the House, that Jack built.

C

THE DOCTOR.

"At his last gasp—as if with opium drugg'd."

DERRY-DOWN TRIANGLE.

"He that sold his country."

THE SPOUTER OF FROTH.

"With merry descants on a nation's woes—
There is a public mischief in his mirth."

THE GUILTY TRIO.

"Great skill have they in *palmistry*, and more
To conjure clean away the gold they touch,
Conveying worthless dross into its place;
Loud when they beg, dumb only when they steal.

    *   *   *   *

———————— Dream after dream ensues;
And still they dream, that they shall still succeed,
And still are disappointed."

This is THE DOCTOR
        of *Circular* fame,
A Driv'ller, a Bigot, a Knave
        without shame:

And *that's* DERRY DOWN TRIANGLE
by name,
From the Land of mis-rule,
and half-hanging, and flame:
And *that* is THE SPOUTER OF FROTH
BY THE HOUR,
The worthless colleague
of their infamous power;
Who dubb'd *him* ' the Doctor'
whom now he calls ' brother',
And, to get at his Place,
took a shot at the other;
Who haunts their *Bad House*,
a base living to earn,
by playing Jack-pudding, and Ruffian,
in turn;
Who bullies, for those
whom he bullied before;
Their *Flash*-man, their Bravo,
a son of a ——;
The hate of the People,
all tatter'd and torn,
Who curse the day
wherein they were born,
On account of Taxation
too great to be borne,
And pray for relief
from night to morn;

Who, in vain, Petition
            in every form,
Who peaceably Meeting,
            to ask for Reform,
Were sabred by Yeomanry Cavalry,
            who,
Were thank'd by THE MAN,
            all shaven and shorn,
All cover'd with Orders—
            and all forlorn ;
THE DANDY OF SIXTY,
            who bows with a grace,
And has *taste* in wigs, collars,
            cuirasses, and lace:
Who to tricksters and fools,
            leaves the State and its treasure,
And, when Britain's in tears,
            sails about at his pleasure:
Who spurn'd from his presence
            the Friends of his youth,
And now has not one
            who will tell him the truth ;
Who took to his counsels, in evil hour,
The Friends to the Reasons of lawless Power ;
That back the Public Informer, who
Would put down the *Thing*, that, in spite of new Acts,
And attempts to restrain it, by Soldiers or Tax,
Will *poison* the Vermin, that plunder the Wealth,
That lay in the House, that Jack built.

——— " Burghers, men immaculate perhaps
In all their private functions, once combin'd,
Become a loathsome body, only fit
For dissolution.
——————— Power usurp'd
Is weakness when oppos'd; conscious of wrong,
'Tis pusillanimous and prone to flight.
——————— I could endure
Chains nowhere patiently; and chains at home,
Where I am free by birthright, not at all."

This **WORD** is the Watchword—

the talisman word,

That the **WATERLOO-MAN** 's to crush

with his sword;

D

But, if shielded by NORFOLK
          and BEDFORD's alliance,
It will set both his sword,
          and him, at defiance;
If FITZWILLIAM, and GROSVENOR, and
          ALBEMARLE aid it,
And assist its best Champions,
          who then dare invade it?
'Tis the terrible WORD OF FEAR,
          night and morn,
To the *Guilty Trio*,
          all cover'd with scorn;
First, to the Doctor,
          of *Circular* fame,
A Driv'ller, a Bigot, a Knave
          without shame:
And next, Derry Down Triangle
          by name,
From the Land of Mis-rule,
          and Half-hanging, and Flame
And then, to the Spouter of Froth
          by the hour,
The worthless Colleague
          of their infamous power;
Who dubb'd *him* ' the Doctor',
          whom now he calls ' brother',
And, to get at his Place,
          took a shot at the other;

Who haunts their *Bad House,*

        a base living to earn,

By playing Jack-Pudding, and Ruffian,

        in turn ;

Who bullies for those,

        whom he bullied before ;

Their *Flash-man*, their Bravo,

        a son of a ———— ;

The hate of the People,

        all tatter'd and torn,

Who curse the day

        wherein they were born

On account of Taxation

        too great to be borne,

And pray for relief,

        from night to morn,

Who in vain Petition

        in every f:rm,

Who peaceably Meeting

        to ask for Reform,

Were sabred by Yeomanry Cavalry,

        who

Were thank'd by THE MAN,

        all shaven and shorn,

All cover'd with Orders—

        and all forlorn ;

THE DANDY OF SIXTY,

        who bows with a grace,

And has *taste* in wigs, collars,
   cuirasses, and lace ;
Who, to tricksters, and fools,
   leaves the State and its treasure,
And, when Britain's in tears
   sails about at his pleasure;
Who spurn'd from his presence
   the Friends of his Youth,
And now has not one
   who will tell him the Truth ;
Who took to his Counsels,
   in evil hour,
The Friends to the Reasons
   of lawless Power ;
That back the Public Informer,
   who
Would put down the Thing,
   that, in spite of new Acts,
And attempts to restrain it
   by Soldiers or Tax,
Will *poison* the Vermin,
That plunder the Wealth,
That lay in the House,
That Jack built.

END OF THE HOUSE THAT JACK BUILT.

THE CLERICAL MAGISTRATE.

" *The Bishop.* Will you be diligent in Prayers—laying aside the study of the world and the flesh ?——*The Priest.* I will.

The Bishop. Will you maintain and set forwards, as much as lieth in you, quietness, peace, and love, among all Christian People ?——*Priest.* I will.

¶ The Bishop laying his hand upon the head of him that receiveth the order of Priesthood, shall say, RECEIVE THE HOLY GHOST."

The Form of Ordination for a Priest.

——— " The pulpit (in the sober use
Of its legitimate peculiar pow'rs)
Must stand acknowledg'd, while the world shall stand,
The most important and effectual guard,
Support, and ornament of virtue's cause.
 *   *   *   *
Behold the picture ! Is it like ?

THIS IS A PRIEST,

made ' according to Law',

Who, on being ordain'd,
            vow'd, by rote, like a daw,
That, he felt himself call'd,
            by the Holy Spirit,
To teach men the Kingdom of Heaven
            to merit;
That, to think of the World and the flesh
            he'd cease,
And keep men in quietness,
            love and peace;
And, making thus his profession
            and boast,
Receiv'd, from the Bishop,
            the Holy Ghost:
Then—not having the fear of God
            before him—
Is sworn in a Justice,
            and one of the *Quorum;*
'Gainst his spiritual Oath,
            puts his Oath of the Bench,
And, instead of his Bible,
            examines a wench;
Gets Chairman of Sessions—leaves his flock,
            sick, or dying,
To license Ale-houses—and assist
            in the trying
Of prostitutes, poachers, pickpockets
            and thieves;——

Having *charged* the Grand Jury,
   dines with them, and gives
" CHURCH AND KING without day-light;"
   gets *fresh*, and puts in—
To the stocks vulgar people
   who fuddle with gin :
Stage coachmen, and toll-men,
   convicts as he pleases ;
And beggars and paupers
   incessantly teazes :
Commits starving vagrants,
   and orders Distress
On the Poor, for their Rates—
   signs warrants to press,
And beats up for names
   to a Loyal Address :
Would indict, for Rebellion,
   those who Petition ;
And, all who look peaceable,
   try for Sedition ;
If the People were legally Meeting,
   in quiet,
Would pronounce it, decidedly—*sec. Stat.*—
   a Riot,
And order the Soldiers
   ' to aid and assist',
That is—kill the helpless,
   Who cannot resist

He, though vowing ' from all worldly studies
to cease',
Breaks the Peace of the Church,
to be Justice of Peace ;
Breaks his vows made to Heaven—
a pander for Power ;
A Perjurer—a guide to the People
no more ;
On God turns his back,
when he turns the State's Agent ;
And damns his own Soul,
to be friends with the ———.

THE END.

" 'Tis Liberty alone, that gives the flow'r
Of fleeting life its lustre and perfume ;
And we are weeds without it."

Printed by W. Hone.
45, Ludgate Hill.

THE REAL

OR

CONSTITUTIONAL HOUSE

THAT

JACK BUILT.

" Look on this PICTURE, and on that."

WITH TWELVE CUTS.

EIGHTH EDITION.

London:

PRINTED FOR J. ASPERNE, CORNHILL;

AND

W. SAMS, St. JAMES's STREET,

1819.
Price One Shilling.

" O England !—model to thy inward greatness
Like little body with a mighty heart,—
What might'st thee do, that honour would thee do,
Were all thy children kind and natural !"

NOTE.

The Mottos are chiefly selected from Shakespeare, Cowper, and Dr. Young.

W. Flint, Printer, Angel Court, Skinner Street.

TO THE

LOVERS OF PEACE,

AND THE

TRUE FRIENDS OF OLD ENGLAND;

TO

ALL THOSE WHO REFUSE TO COUNTENANCE

Political Parties, Oratorical Demagogues, and Public and Private Writers,

WHO AFFECT TO SHOW THEIR

PATRIOTISM AND ZEAL FOR THEIR COUNTRY,

BY AIMING TO DEGRADE

HER BEST INSTITUTIONS;

AND

BY LIBELLING HER IMMORTAL

DEFENDERS,

THIS

EFFUSION OF A MOMENT,

IS MOST

RESPECTFULLY INSCRIBED, BY THEIR FELLOW-LABOURER IN THE GOOD CAUSE OF

SOCIAL ORDER,

THE AUTHOR.

London, December 13th, 1819.

"England, with all thy faults, I love thee still——
——————— and, while yet a nook is left,
Where English minds and manners may be found,
Shall be constrain'd to love thee ——————— "

THIS IS

THE HOUSE
THAT JACK BUILT.

"Incomparable gem! thy worth untold;
Cheap, tho' blood-bought, and thrown away when sold;
May no foes ravish thee, and no false friend
Betray thee, while professing to defend!
Prize it, ye ministers; ye monarchs spare;
Ye patriots guard it with a miser's care."

THE TREASURES

that lay
In the HOUSE that Jack built.

B

"I'the commonwealth I would by contraries
Execute all things: for no kind of traffick
Would I admit; no name of magistrate;
Letters should not be known; no use of service,
Of riches or of poverty; no contracts,
Successions; bound of land, tilth, vineyard, none:
No use of metal, corn, or wine, or oil;
No occupation; all men idle, all;
And women too; but innocent and pure:
No sovereignty:— *   *   * - *   *
All things in common nature should produce
Without sweat or endeavour: treason, felony."

"The Thieves are scatter'd, and possess'd with fear
So strongly, that they dare not meet each other."

THESE ARE

THE THIEVES

Who would plunder the TREASURES
That lay in the HOUSE
That Jack built.

"Thou, as a gallant bark from Albion's coast
(The storms all weather'd and the ocean cross'd)
Shoots into port at some well-haven'd isle,
Where spices breathe, and brighter seasons smile;
Where sits quiescent on the floods that show
Her beauteous form reflected clear below,
While airs impregnated with incense play
Around her, fanning light her streamers gay;
So thou, with sails how swift! hast reach'd the shore,
Where tempests never beat nor billows roar."

THIS IS

"THE PILOT

that weather'd the Storm,"
And devised the means of subduing
THE THIEVES,
Who would plunder the TREASURES
That lay in the HOUSE that Jack built.

"Such men are rais'd to station and command,
When Providence means mercy to a land.
He speaks, and they appear ; to Him they owe
Skill to direct, and strength to strike the blow ;
To manage with address, to seize with pow'r
The crisis of a dark decisive hour."

THESE ARE
THE PATRIOTS
of high renown—
The Heroes of Britain—the Gems of her Crown ;
Who, despising all Danger, and scorning all Fear,
When all was at stake, that their Country held dear,
'Midst Jacobin Rebels, and Friends of Reform,
Supported " THE PILOT
that weather'd the Storm,"
Who devised the means, of subduing
THE THIEVES,
Who would plunder the TREASURES
That lay in the HOUSE that Jack built.

" Go to, they are not men o'their words."

———— " Having wielded the elements, and built
A thousand systems—each in his own way,
They should go out in fume, and be forgot."

" Like quicksilver, the rhet'ric they display
Shines as it runs, but grasp'd, it slips away."

" Patriots are grown too shrew'd to be sincere,
And we too wise to trust them ————"

THESE ARE

THE HYPOCRITES,

shaven and shorn—
The broad-bottom'd Whigs, now all forlorn ;

Who grumbl'd and growl'd, from night till morn,
And pointed " the slow-moving finger of scorn,"
At the Country in which they were all " bred and
     born,"
Had grown saucy and fat, on its wine and its corn ;
Who blew a loud blast, on the place-hunter's horn,
And with Joe Millar's Jests, did their Speeches adorn ;
Who predicted the final success of our foes,
Then sigh'd if they sunk, and rejoic'd if they rose ;
Who swore, when the French were defeated, that we
Were kill'd by the sword, or were drown'd in the
     Sea ;
Who rail'd against Placemen, till *they* were in Place,
Then sneer'd at their Monarch—nay, laugh'd in his
     face ;
Who bragg'd of their Talents, and pass'd a few Acts ;
And increas'd, *5 per Cent.* the vile Property Tax ;
Who thought themselves safe in their snug little
     birth,
And gave themselves up to Carousing and Mirth ;
Who slept every night, upon Pillows of Down,
    Abhorring those PATRIOTS, of
       high renown—
The Heroes of Britain—the Gems of her Crown ;
Who, despising all Dangers, and scorning all Fear,
When all was at stake, that their Country held dear,
'Midst Jacobin Rebels, and Friends of Reform,
    Supported " THE PILOT
       that weather'd the Storm ;"
Who devised the means, of subduing
    THE THIEVES,
Who would plunder the TREASURES
That lay in the HOUSE that Jack built.

———— " Poverty with most, who whimper forth
Their long complaints, is self-inflicted woe ;
The effects of laziness or sottish waste."

THE MAJOR.
" O, Sir, you are old ;
Nature in you stands on the very verge
Of her confine : you should be rul'd and led
By some discretion, that discerns your state
Better than you yourself ————— "

ORATOR HUNT.
" There shall be, in England, seven half-penny loaves sold for a penny ;
the three-hooped pot shall have ten hoops ; and I will make it felony to
drink small beer : all the realm shall be in common, and in Cheapside shall
my palfry go to grass. And, when I am king, there shall be no money ; all
shall eat and drink on my score ; and I will apparel them all in one livery,
that they may agree like brothers, and worship me their lord "
" The first thing we do, let's kill all the lawyers."

CARLILE.
" And is there, who the blessed Cross wipes off,
As a foul blot from his dishonour'd brow,
If Angels tremble, 'tis at such a sight."

THESE ARE
THE RADICALS—
Friends of Reform,

Devising new Plots for exciting a Storm :
A mistaken old MAJOR sits hatching Sedition,
Yet dreams all the while of a lawful Petition ;
And whilst Orator HUNT indites the Inscription,
He pockets the Pence of the Penny Subscription ;
Yet vows he's the best, and most honest of men,
Swears lies to the LAWYER, who swears them
   again.
And here is the DOCTOR of Spa-Fields fame,
Who vow'd he would set all the Town in a flame,
With a Stocking well-stuff'd full of Powder and Ball,
A Speech of two hours, and a Pistol withal.
Here's PRESTON, the Cobbler, just come from
   his trial,
To Gin and Sedition outrageously loyal ;
Like most of his breth'ren, who, spite of their votes,
Preserve their allegiance to Thompson and Coates ;
And would sooner expel from their Clubs and their
   Lodges,
The Chairman himself, than Friends—Henley and
   Hodges,
Here's THISTLEWOOD, too, who tells " Tales
   out of School,"
That Orator HUNT is a Knave and a Fool.
A Staffordshire BARONET, wrapp'd in a scarf,
   Sits nursing an ugly, mis-shapen,
    BLACK DWARF.
And here is CARLILE, with his Two-penny
   Treason,
Who prefers to his Bible the vile " Age of Reason ;"
Who " wipes off the Cross," as an infamous stain,
Despises his Saviour, but worships Tom Paine.
These are all ragged RADICALS, tatter'd and torn,
Who better, by far, had never been born,
On account of their Treasons, too great to be borne,

First hatch'd by the HYPOCRITES,
shaven and shorn—
The broad-bottom'd Whigs, now all forlorn ;
Who grumbl'd and growl'd, from night till morn,
And pointed the " slow-moving finger of scorn,"
At the Country in which they were all " bred and
born,"
Had grown saucy and fat, on its wine and its corn ;
Who blew a loud blast, on the place-hunter's horn,
And with Joe Millar's Jests, did their Speeches
adorn ;
Who predicted the final success of our foes,
Then sigh'd if they sunk, and rejoic'd if they rose ;
Who swore, when the French were defeated, that we
Were kill'd by the sword, or were drown'd in the
Sea ;
Who rail'd against Placemen, till *they* were in Place,
Then sneer'd at their Monarch—nay, laugh'd in his
face ;
Who bragg'd of their Talents, and pass'd a few Acts,
And increas'd, *5 per Cent.* the vile Property Tax ;
Who thought themselves safe in their snug little birth,
And gave themselves up, to Carousing and Mirth ;
Who slept ev'ry night, upon Pillows of Down,
Abhorring those PATRIOTS,
of high renown—
The Heroes of Britain—the Gems of her Crown ;
Who, despising all Danger, and scorning all Fear,
When all was at stake, that their Country held dear,
'Midst Jacobin Rebels, and Friends of Reform,
Supported " THE PILOT
that weather'd the Storm,"
Who devised the means of subduing
THE THIEVES,
Who would plunder the TREASURES
That lay in the HOUSE that Jack built.
c

" This is some fellow,
Who, having been prais'd for his bluntness, doth affect
A saucy roughness — —— —— ——
These kind of knaves I know, which in this plainness
Harbour more craft, and more corrupter ends,
Than twenty silly ducking observants,
That stretch their duties nicely."

" As one, who lay in thickets and in brakes
Entangl'd, winds now this way and now that
His devious course uncertain, seeking home."

THIS IS

WILL COBBETT,

with Thomas Paine's bones,

A bag full of brick-bats, and
one full of stones,
With which he intends to discharge
the long Debt
He owes to his Friends, and
Sir Francis Burdett :
'Tis Cobbett, the changeling,
the worthless and base,
Just arriv'd from New York, with
his impudent face,
Who comes to dispel our
political fogs,
And to add one more beast to
our Hampshire Hogs,
To mix with the RADICALS—
FRIENDS OF REFORM,
Devising new Plots, for
exciting a Storm :
A mistaken old Major sits hatching Sedition,
Yet dreams all the while of a lawful Petition ;
And whilst Orator Hunt indites the Inscription,
He pockets the Pence of the Penny Subscription ;
Yet vows he's the best, and most honest of men,
Swears lies to the Lawyer, who swears them again.
And here is the Doctor, of Spa-Fields fame,
Who vow'd he would set all the Town in a flame,
With a Stocking well-stuff'd full of Powder and Ball,
A Speech of two hours, and a Pistol withal.
Here's Preston, the Cobbler, just come from his trial,
To Gin and Sedition outrageously loyal ;
Like most of his breth'ren, who, spite of their
votes,
Preserve their allegiance to Thompson and Coates;

And would sooner expel from their Clubs and their
    Lodges,
The Chairman himself, than friends Henley and
    Hodges.
Here's Thistlewood, too, who tells " Tales out of
    School,"
        That Orator Hunt is
                a Knave and a Fool.
A Staffordshire Baronet,
                wrapp'd in a scarf,
Sits nursing an ugly,
                mis-shapen, Black Dwarf.
And here is Carlile, with his
                Two-penny Treason,
Who prefers to his Bible,
                the vile " Age of Reason;"
Who " wipes off the Cross,"
                as an infamous stain,
Despises his Saviour, but
                worships Tom Paine.
These are all ragged Radicals,
                tatter'd and torn,
Who better, by far, had
                never been born,
On account of their Treasons,
                too great to be borne,
First hatched by the HYPOCRITES
                shaven and shorn—
The broad-bottom'd Whigs,
                now all forlorn ;
Who grumbl'd and growl'd, from night till morn,
And pointed the " slow-moving finger of scorn,"

At the Country in which they were all " bred and
    born,"
Had grown saucy and fat, on its wine and its corn ;
Who blew a loud blast on the place-hunter's horn,
And with Joe Millar's Jests did their Speeches
    adorn ;
Who predicted the final success of our foes,
Then sigh'd if they sunk ; and rejoic'd if they rose ;
Who swore, when the French were defeated, that we
Were kill'd by the sword, or were drown'd in the
    Sea ;
Who rail'd against Placemen, till *they* were in Place,
Then sneer'd at their Monarch—nay, laugh'd in his
    face ;
Who bragg'd of their Talents, and pass'd a few Acts,
And increas'd, *5 per Cent.* the vile Property Tax ;
Who thought themselves safe, in their snug little
    birth,
And gave themselves up, to Carousing and Mirth ;
Who slept every night, upon Pillows of Down,
        Abhorring those PATRIOTS,
                    of high renown—
The Heroes of Britain—the Gems of her Crown ;
Who, despising all Danger, and scorning all Fear,
When all was at stake, that their Country held dear,
'Midst Jacobin Rebels, and Friends of Reform,
        Supported " THE PILOT
                that weather'd the Storm,"
    Who devised the means of subduing
            THE THIEVES,
Who would plunder the TREASURES
That lay in the HOUSE that Jack built.

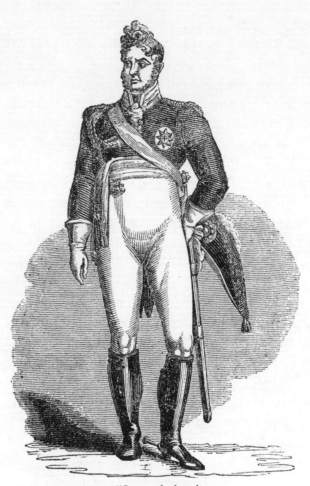

———— — " In speech, in gait,
In diet, in affections of delight,
In military rules, humours of blood,
He was the mark and glass, copy and book,
That fashion'd others."

———

" Methought, thy very gait did prophecy
A royal nobleness :—I must embrace thee ;
Let sorrow split my heart, if ever
I did hate thee, or thy FATHER !"

———————————

THIS IS

THE PRINCE

of a generous Mind,

The Friend of his Country, and
all Mankind;
Who, lending his Ear to
the dictates of Truth,
Dismiss'd from his presence
the Friends of his Youth;
Who took to his Councils
in fortunate hour,
The foes to Napoleon's
exorbitant power;
Who views with disdain, or
a good-humour'd smile,
The libellous trash of the
base and the vile;
And all such as COBBETT, with
Thomas Paine's Bones,
A bag full of brick-bats, and one full of stones,
With which he intends to discharge the long Debt
He owes to his Friends, and Sir Francis Burdett.
'Tis Cobbett, the changeling, the worthless and base,
Just arrived from New York, with his impudent face,
Who comes to dispel, our Political fogs,
And to add one more beast to our Hampshire Hogs,
To mix with the RADICALS—
Friends of Reform,
Devising new Plots for exciting a Storm:
A mistaken old Major sits hatching Sedition,
Yet dreams all the while of a lawful Petition;
And whilst Orator Hunt indites the Inscription,
He pockets the Pence of the Penny Subscription;
Yet vows he's the best, and most honest of men,
Swears lies to the Lawyer, who swears them again.

And here is the Doctor of Spa-Fields fame,
Who vow'd he would set all the Town in a flame,
With a Stocking well-stuff'd full of Powder and Ball,
A Speech of two hours, and a Pistol withal.
Here's Preston, the Cobbler, just come from his trial,
To Gin and Sedition outrageously loyal;
Like most of his breth'ren, who, spite of their votes,
Preserve their allegiance to Thompson and Coates:
And would sooner expel from their Clubs and their
      Lodges,
The Chairman himself, than friends Henley and
      Hodges.
Here's Thistlewood, too, who tells " Tales out of
      School,"
That Orator Hunt is a Knave and a Fool.
A Staffordshire Baronet, wrapp'd in a scarf,
Sits nursing an ugly, mis-shapen, Black Dwarf.
And here is Carlile, with his Two-penny Treason,
Who prefers to his Bible the vile " Age of Reason ;"
Who " wipes off the Cross," as an infamous stain,
Despises his Saviour, but worships Tom Paine.
These are all ragged Radicals, tatter'd and torn,
Who, better by far, had never been born,
On account of their Treasons, too great to be borne,
    First hatch'd by the HYPOCRITES,
        shaven and shorn—
The broad-bottom'd Whigs, now all forlorn ;
Who grumbl'd and growl'd, from night till morn,
And pointed the " slow-moving finger of scorn,"
At the Country in which they were all " bred and
      born,"
Had grown saucy and fat, on its wine and its corn ;

Who blew a loud blast, on the place-hunter's horn,
And with Joe Millar's Jests did their Speeches adorn;
Who predicted the final success of our foes,
Then sigh'd if they sunk, and rejoic'd if they rose;
Who swore, when the French were defeated, that we
Were kill'd by the sword, or were drown'd in the
  Sea;
Who rail'd against Placemen, till *they* were in Place,
Then sneer'd at their Monarch—nay, laugh'd in his
  face;
Who bragg'd of their Talents, and pass'd a few Acts,
And increas'd, *5 per Cent.* the vile Property Tax;
Who thought themselves safe, in their snug little
  birth,
And gave themselves up to Carousing and Mirth;
Who slept ev'ry night, upon Pillows of Down,
  Abhorring those PATRIOTS,
    of high renown—
The Heroes of Britain—the Gems of her Crown;
Who, despising all Danger, and scorning all Fear,
When all was at stake, that their Country held dear,
'Midst Jacobin Rebels, and Friends of Reform,
  Supported " THE PILOT
    that weather'd the Storm,"
Who devised the means of subduing
  THE THIEVES,
Who would plunder the TREASURES
That lay in the HOUSE that Jack built.

END OF THE HOUSE THAT JACK BUILT.

D

"I venerate the man, whose heart is warm,
Whose hands are pure, whose doctrine, and whose life
Coincident, exhibit lucid proof
That he is honest in the SACRED CAUSE."

THIS IS

A PRIEST

made according to Truth,
The guide of Old Age—
the Instructor of Youth;

Belov'd and respected by all
      whom he teaches,
Himself the example of
      all that he preaches ;
The friend of the poor,
      the afflicted and sad,
The terror alone of the
      impious and bad.
He embroils not himself
      with affairs of the State,
And, though closely alli'd,
      keeps aloof from the great ;
Yet ne'er will against them
      vile calumnies fling ;
But, fearing his Maker,
      he honours his King.
A radical friend to
      the Cause of Reform—
A true Revolutionist,
      loving a storm :—
A storm of the soul—
      a Reform of the heart,—
A radical change, that
      bids error depart,
He harangues to the people,
      like Prophets of old ;
But harangues not for
      popular favour nor gold.
Obedient to all the commands of his Lord,
Knows how to distinguish the Bible and Sword.
His greatest delight is to teach and do good ;
His greatest abhorrence the shedding of blood ;

Hence he cautions the thoughtless, of those to
    beware,
Who affect for the poor and the needy to care,
Yet feed not the hungry, nor cover the bare ;
Who prate about Liberty, Virtue, and Reason,
Whilst plotting Destruction, Rebellion, and Treason;
And pretending at once to destroy Superstition,
Lead their blind-folded votaries headlong to perdition.
Against these blasphemers and hollow deceivers,
This "Priest of the Temple," warns all true believers,
Exhorting the poor to hold fast by the Bible,
And leave all the rest to the children of libel ;
To look up to Him to whom mercy belongs,
To protect them from ill, and redress all their wrongs;
Assur'd of this truth, that we read in the word :
" They shall ne'er be forsaken who trust in the
    LORD."

W. Flint, Printer, Angel Court, Skinner Street.

MAN IN THE MOON

&c. &c. &c.

" If Cæsar can hide the Sun with a blanket, or put the Moon in his pocket, we
will pay him tribute for light."   *Cymbeline.*

WITH FIFTEEN CUTS.

Eighteenth Edition.

LONDON:
PRINTED BY AND FOR WILLIAM HONE,
45, LUDGATE HILL.
1820.

ONE SHILLING.

——— ——— " Is there not
Some hidden thunder in the stores of heaven,
Red with uncommon wrath, to blast the men
Who owe their greatness to their country's ruin?"

Dedicated

TO THE

RIGHT HON. GEORGE CANNING,

AUTHOR OF PARODIES ON SCRIPTURE, TO RIDICULE
HIS POLITICAL OPPONENTS; AND COLLEAGUE
WITH THE PROSECUTORS OF
POLITICAL PARODY:

WHO,

AFTER LAMPOONING LORD SIDMOUTH, AND HOLDING HIM UP TO
THE SCORN AND CONTEMPT OF ALL ENGLAND, AS A CHARLATAN
AND "PRIME DOCTOR TO THE COUNTRY," NOW TAKES
A SUBORDINATE PART UNDER HIM AS
A "PRIME" MINISTER:

WHO,

AFTER DENOUNCING LORD CASTLEREAGH'S INCAPACITY FOR
INFERIOR OFFICE, AND CONFIRMING THAT DENUNCIATION BY HIS
PISTOLS, ACCEPTED INFERIOR OFFICE HIMSELF UNDER THE
CONTROL OF THAT VERY LORD CASTLEREAGH; AND
SEEKS TO PROLONG HIS POLITICAL EXISTENCE
BY THE FAWNING BLANDISHMENT OF "MY
NOBLE FRIEND," ALTHOUGH THAT
"NOBLE FRIEND" HAS NOT BEEN
OBSERVED TO ENCOURAGE
THE EMBARRASSING ENDEARMENT,
BY RETURNING IT:

THUS,

BY HIS PARODIES,
HIS PISTOLS, AND HIS WITS,
FIGHTING AND WRITING HIS WAY
TO PLACE AND PROFIT UNDER MINISTERS,
WHOM THE DERISION OF HIS PEN
HAS DRIVEN TO THE MISERY
OF HIS ALLIANCE.

———

THE

MAN IN THE MOON,

A SPEECH FROM THE THRONE,

TO THE SENATE OF LUNATARIA

In the Moon.

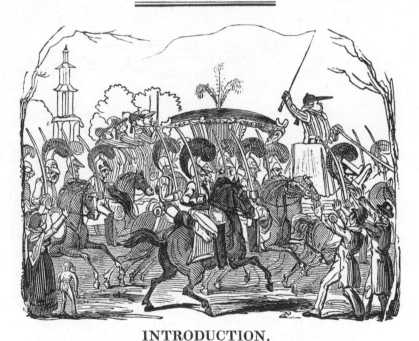

INTRODUCTION.

I LATELY dream'd that, in a huge balloon,
All silk and gold, I journey'd to the Moon,
Where the same objects seem'd to meet my eyes
That I had lately left below the skies;

And judge of my astonishment, on seeing
All things exactly, to a hair, agreeing :
The mountains, rivers, cities, trees, and towers,
On Cynthia's silver surface, seem'd like ours ;
Men, women, children, language, dress, and faces,
Lords, Commons, Lackies, Pensioners, and Places,
Whigs, Tories, Lawyers, Priests, and men of blood,
And even *Radicals*—by all that's good!

In a long street, just such as London's Strand is,
'Midst Belles, and Beggars, Pickpockets, and Dandies,
Onward I went, between a brazen horse,
And a large Inn which bore a Golden Cross,
Then through a passage, narrow, long and dark,
That brought my footsteps to a spacious park,

It chanc'd that morning that the Sovereign Dey,
The Prince of Lunataria, pass'd that way—
Gods! what a sight! what countless crouds were there,
What yells, and groans, and hootings, rent the air!
By which, I learn'd, the Lunatarian nation
Are wont to testify their admiration;
We dont do so on earth—but that's no matter—
The Dey went onward, midst a hideous clatter
To meet the Senators; for 'twas appointed,
That, on that morning, He—the Lord's anointed—
Should make a grand Oration from the throne,
That his most royal pleasure might be known

Respecting certain great affairs of State:—
I heard the speech; Oh! could the Muse relate
The "*elegance,*" the sweet "*distinctiveness,*"
With which his Royal Deyship did address
That reverend body of Moonarian sages,
I'd write a book that should endure for ages.
Alas! such heights are not for me to reach;
I'll, therefore, from my note-book, take the Speech,
And you must say, as 'tis by Pope exprest,
"Give all thou canst, and *we* will dream the rest!"

———

THE SPEECH.

—

MY L—rds and G—tl——n,
      I grieve to say,
    That poor old Dad,
    Is just as—bad,
  As when I met you here
     the other day.

'Tis pity that these cursed State Affairs
Should take you from your pheasants and your hares
          Just now:
          But lo!
CONSPIRACY and TREASON are abroad!
Those imps of darkness, gender'd in the wombs
Of spinning-jennies, winding-wheels, and looms,
          In Lunashire—
          Oh, Lord!
My L—ds and G—tl—n, we've much to fear!

Reform, Reform, the swinish rabble cry—
Meaning, of course, rebellion, blood, and riot—
Audacious rascals! you, my Lords, and I,
Know 'tis their duty to be starved in quiet:
But they have grumbling habits, incompatible
With the repose of *our* august community—
They see that good things are with *us* come-at-ible,
And therefore slyly watch their opportunity
          To get a share;
          Yes, they declare
That we are not God's favorites alone—
That *they* have rights to food, and clothes, and air,
As well as you, the Brilliants of a throne!
Oh! indications foul of revolution—
The villains would destroy the Constitution!

I've given orders for a lot of Letters,
From these seditious, scribbling, scoundrels' betters,
N—d—n and N—rr—s, F—ch—r, W—t and H—y,
    'To *lie*, for your instruction,'
      Upon the table:
From which said premises you'll soon be able
      To make a fair deduction,
That some decisive measures must be taken,
      Without delay,
    To quell the *Radicals,*
      and save our bacon.

And now, my faithful C—m—ns,
      You must find
      The means to raise the wind:
For Derry Down, and Sid, have thought it wise,
To have—*besides the Spies*—
A few more Cut-throats, to protect the rhino
Of loyal people,—such as you and I know.

Van's estimates will come before you straight;
      And, I foresee
That your opinions will with mine agree,
      No lighter weight
    Can well be placed on

          c

JOHNNY MOON CALF'S back,
Who is, you know,
              a very willing hack.
    The revenue has fluctuated
              slightly—
         See the *Courier*—
But it's been found to be
         improving nightly—
For two weeks past,—
              therefore we've nought to fear.
    Some branches of our trade
         are still deprest,
And those dependant on them
         wanting food,

But that's a sort of
>> *temporary evil—*
'Twill wear away:
>> perhaps 'tis for the best :—
At all events, 'twill do
>> no good
To let the starving wretches
>> be uncivil.

Five years, ago you know,
>> our sad condition
Was partly owing to
>> ' *the quick transition*
From war to peace'—then,
>> we had ' *scanty crops*'—
Then, something else—and now—
>> our weavers' shops
Are full of *Radicals,*
>> and *Flags,* and *Caps ;*
But '*temporary*' still
>> are these mishaps—
The ' quick transition's' gone,
>> the 'crops' are good,
And though the *Radicals*
>> may still want food,
A few

STEEL LOZENGES

will stop their pain,
And set the Constitution
right again.

My L—ds and G—tl—n,
The foreign powers
Write me word frequently
that they are ours,
Most truly and sincerely,
in compliance
With our most

HOLY COMPACT AND ALLIANCE,

The purposes of which
      I need not mention—
You that have brains can guess
      at the intention.

'Tis my most axious wish,
      now we're at peace,
That all eternal discontents
      should cease—
T' accomplish which
      I see no better way
Than putting one-eyed pensioners
      on full pay.

'The body of the people, I do think,
        are loyal still,'
But pray My L—ds and G—tl—n,
        don't shrink
From exercising all your care
        and skill,
Here, and at home,
    TO CHECK THE CIRCULATION

OF LITTLE BOOKS,

Whose very looks—
Vile *'two-p'nny trash,'*
        bespeak abomination.
Oh! they are full of blasphemies
        and libels,
And people read them
        oftener than their bibles

Go H—df—t, Y—rm—th, C—le—gh, and C—nn—g,
           Go, and be planning,
Within your virtuous minds, what best will answer
To save *our* morals from this public cancer;
Go and impress, my friends, upon all classes,
From sleek-fac'd Swindlers down to half-starv'd Asses,
'That, from religious principles alone,'
(*Don't be such d—d fools as to blab your own*),
Temperance, chasteness, conjugal attention—
With other virtues that I need not mention—
And from subordination, and respect,
To every knave in robes of office deck'd—
'Can they expect to gain divine protection'
And save their sinful bodies from dissection!

His Highness ceased—
       The dissonance of Babel
Rose from the motley
       Moonitarian rabble :
The yell of loyalty—
       the dungeon groan—
The shriek of woe—
       the starving infant's moan—
The brazen trumpets' note—
       the din of war—
The shouts of freemen
       rising from afar—
Darted in horrid discord
       through my brain :—
I woke, and found myself
       on Earth again.

A POLITICAL

CHRISTMAS CAROL,

Set to Music,

TO BE CHAUNTED OR SUNG

THROUGHOUT THE UNITED KINGDOM AND THE

DOMINIONS BEYOND THE SEAS,

BY ALL PERSONS

THEREUNTO ESPECIALLY MOVED.

" Go draw your quills, and draw *five Bills*,

" Put out yon blaze of light."—

Carol.

THE CAROL.

To be Sung exactly as set.

God rest you mer - ry Gen - tle - men, let no-thing you dis-

may; Re - mem - ber we were left a - live up - on last Christ mas

day, With both our lips at li - ber - ty to praise Lord

C————————h, For his prac-ti- cal com-fort and

joy, And joy: For his prac - ti-cal com - fort and joy!

He ' turn'd his back upon himself'
    And straight to ' Lunnun' came,
To two two-sided Lawyers
    With tidings of the same,
That our own land must ' prostrate stand'
    Unless we praise his name—
      For his ' practical' comfort and joy!

"Go fear not," said his L————p
    " Let nothing you affright;
" Go draw your quills, and draw *five Bills,*
    " Put out yon blaze of light:
" I'm able to advance you,
    " Go *stamp* it out then quite—
      " And give me some ' features' of joy!"

The Lawyers at those tidings
  Rejoiced much in mind,
And left their friends a staring
  To go and raise the wind,
And straight went to the Taxing-men
  And said "the Bills come find—
    "For 'fundamental' comfort and joy!"

The Lawyers found majorities
  To do as they did say,
They found them at their mangers
  Like oxen at their hay,
Some *lying,* and some kneeling down,
  All to L——d C———h
    For his 'practical' comfort and joy!

With sudden joy and gladness
  Rat G—ff—d was beguiled,
They each sat at his L———p's side,
  He patted them and smiled ;
Yet C—pl—y, on his nether end,
  Sat like a *new born* Child,—
    But without either comfort or joy!

He thought upon his Father,
  His virtues, and his fame,
And how that father hoped from him
  For glory to his name,
And as his chin dropp'd on his breast,
  His pale cheeks burn'd with shame :—
    He'll never more know comfort or joy!

Lord C———h doth rule yon *House,*
   And all who there do reign;
They've let us live *this* Christmas time—
   D'ye think they will again?
They say they are our masters—
   That's neither *here,* nor *there:*
      God send us all a happy new year!

END OF THE CAROL.

"THE DOCTOR"

"His name's the Doctor."

A PARODY WRITTEN BY THE RIGHT HONORABLE

GEORGE CANNING, M. P.

Lord FOLKESTONE confessed that there had been a smile on his countenance at one part of the right honorable gentleman (Mr. CANNING)'s speech, and it seemed to him very extraordinary, even after the reconciliation that had taken place, to hear the right honorable gentleman stand up for the talents of that poor "Doctor" (Lord SIDMOUTH), who has so long been the butt of his most bitter and unsparing ridicule *(loud laughter and shouts of hear, hear)*. Whether in poetry or prose, the great object of his derision, and that for want of ability and sense, was the noble lord whom he (Mr. CANNING) had so strenuously defended that night; and now forsooth, he wondered that any person could object to confide unlimited power in the hands of a person, according to his own former opinions, so likely to be duped and misled *(hear, hear)*. Yes, the house would remember the lines in which, at different times, the right honorable gentleman (Mr. CANNING), had been pleased to panegyrize his (Mr. CANNING's) noble *friend* (Lord SIDMOUTH) of which the following were not the worst:—

"I showed myself *prime Doctor* to the country;
My ends attain'd, my only aim has been
To keep my place, and gild my humble name."—
(A loud laugh)

Yes, this was the view the right honorable gentleman had once drawn of his noble friend, who was *then* described by him thus:—

"My name's the Doctor—on the Berkshire hills," &c.
[*See the Parody below for the remainder of Lord Folkestone's Quotation—For his Lordship's Speech, see* Evans's Debates, 1817, p. 1568.]

My name's THE DOCTOR ; *on the Berkshire hills*
My father purged his patients—a wise man,
Whose constant care was to increase his store,
And keep his eldest son—myself—at home.
But *I had heard of Politics, and long'd*
To sit within the Commons' House, and get
A place, and luck gave what my sire denied.

103

Some thirteen years ago, or ere my fingers
Had learn'd to mix a potion, or to bleed,
I flatter'd Pitt ; I cring'd, and sneak'd and fawnd,
And thus became the Speaker.   I alone,
With pompous gait, and peruke full of wisdom,
Th' unruly members could control, or call
The House to order.

    Tir'd of the Chair, I sought a bolder flight,
And, grasping at his power, I struck my friend,
Who held that place which now I've made my own.
Proud of my triumph, I disdain'd to court
The patron hand which fed me—or to seem
Grateful to him who rais'd me into notice.
And, when the King had call'd his Parliament
To meet him here conven'd in Westminster,
With all my fam'ly crowding at my heels,
My brothers, cousins, followers and my son,
I show'd myself PRIME DOCTOR to the country.

    My ends attain'd my only aim has been
To keep my place—and gild my humble name !

" Brother, brother, we are both in the wrong !"—*Peach'em and Lockit.*

END OF "THE DOCTOR."

TO THE READER.

THE AUTHOR OF THE POLITICAL HOUSE THAT JACK BUILT, perceiving the multitude of attempts at Imitation and Imposture, occasioned by the unparalleled sale of that Jeu d'Esprit, in justice to the public and to himself, respectfully states, that, induced by nearly forty years of the most confidential intimacy with Mr. HONE, and by the warmest friendship and affection for him and his family, he originally selected him for his publisher exclusively; that he has not suffered, nor will he suffer, a line of his writing to pass into the hands of any other Bookseller; and that his last, and owing to imperative claims upon his pen of a higher order, possibly his very last production, in that way, will be found in the MAN IN THE MOON.

Sale Extraordinary.

FREEHOLD PUBLIC HOUSES;

Divided into Lots for the convenience of Purchasers.

TO BE SOLD by Mr. HONE, at his House, No. 45, Ludgate Hill, THIS DAY, and following days until entirely disposed of,

AN EXTENSIVE UNENCUMBERED FREEHOLD PROPERTY in separate Lots. Each comprising a Capital well accustomed bustling Free Public House, most desirably situated, being thoroughly established in the very heart of England, and called by the Name or Sign of "The House that Jack Built." Served Forty Thousand Customers in the last Six Weeks. Draws the Choicest Spirits, and is not in the mixing or *whine* way.

The Feathers and Wellington Arms combining to injure this property by setting up Houses of Ill Fame, under the same sign, the Public are cautioned against them; they are easily known from the original House by their Customers being few in number, and of a description better understood than expressed.

The present is an undeniable opportunity to persons wishing to improve their affairs, or desirous of entering into the public line; there being no Fixtures and the Coming-in easy.

Immediate possession will be given in consideration of One Shilling of good and lawful money of the Realm, paid to any of the Booksellers of the United Kingdom.

*** May be viewed; and Particulars had as above.

UNIVERSITY LITERATURE.—With Thirteen Cuts, price 1s.

THE FORTY FOURTH EDITION OF THE POLITICAL HOUSE THAT JACK BUILT.

₊ This Publication was entered at Stationers' Hall, and Copies were duly delivered, according to Act of Parliament, one being for the British Museum; yet it is held in such estimation by all ranks, from the mansion to the cottage, including men of high classical and literary attainment, that it is coveted by eminent and learned bodies for the purpose of being preserved and deposited in the other National Libraries, as appears by the following notice:—

(COPY.)　　　　　　London, Jan. 26, 1820.

SIR—I am authorised and requested to demand of you nine copies of the under-mentioned Work—THE POLITICAL HOUSE THAT JACK BUILT—for the use of the following Libraries and Universities :—Bodleian; Cambridge; Sion College; Edinburgh; Advocates' Library, Edinburgh; Glasgow; Aberdeen; St. Andrew's; Trinity College, and the King's Inns, Dublin.　　I am, Sir, your obedient servant,

GEORGE GREENHILL,

Warehouse-keeper to the Company of Stationers.

To Mr. WM. HONE, Ludgate-hill.

This "authorized" and official "demand" on behalf of the Universities and Public Libraries, was immediately complied with; and to save those distinguished bodies the trouble of a similar application for "THE MAN IN THE MOON," copies of that work were also sent with the copies of the Political House that Jack Built, so demanded " for their use."

†₊† A SUPERIOR EDITION OF THE POLITICAL HOUSE THAT JACK BUILT, is now published, printed on fine Vellum Drawing Paper, with the Cuts handsomely COLOURED, Price 3s.—The same Edition plain, Price 2s.

Withdrawn from the Press,

A LETTER TO THE SOLICITOR GENERAL.
By WILLIAM HONE.

₊ Since the announcement of this Publication, the attack of the Solicitor-General upon the Juries of my Country has drawn down upon that Gentleman, within the walls of Parliament, such deserved animadversion as to render superfluous any interference on my part.

Two years have elapsed since I broke away from the toils; and it seems the escape of the destined victim is never to be forgiven! The cause of which the Solicitor-General is unexpectedly the gratuitous advocate, has taken appropriate refuge in the snug precincts of Gatton. There let it wither!

The verdicts of my Juries require no other vindication than a faithful recital of the grounds on which they were founded. From the period at which those verdicts were pronounced, and with a view to that vindication, I have been unremittingly employed in the collection and arrangement of rare and curious materials which the Solicitor-General's attack will induce me to extend to

A COMPLETE HISTORY OF PARODY.

This History I purpose to bring out, very speedily, with extensive graphic illustrations, and I flatter myself it will answer the various purposes of satisfying the expectations of my numerous and respectable subscribers—of justifying my own motives in publishing the Parodies—of throwing a strong light upon the presumable motives of my prosecutors in singling me out from my Noble and Right Honorable Fellow Parodists—of holding up Trial by Jury to the encreased love and veneration of the British People—and above all, of making every calumny upon the verdicts of three successive, honorable and intelligent Juries recoil upon the slanderer, be he who he may, that dares to asperse them.　　　　　　　　　　　　　　　　　　　　　　　　　W. HONE.

Ludgate-hill, March. 1820.

Printed by W. Hone,
45, Ludgate Hill.

Third Edition.

THE

LOYAL
MAN IN THE MOON.

WITH THIRTEEN CUTS.

o

BY THE AUTHOR OF
THE CONSTITUTIONAL HOUSE THAT JACK BUILT.

LONDON:
PRINTED FOR C. CHAPPLE, 66, PALL MALL,
Bookseller to His Majesty, and His Royal Highness the Duke of York,
AND J. JOHNSTON, CHEAPSIDE.

1820.

[Price One Shilling.] 107

W. Shackell, Printer, Johnson's-court, Fleet-street, London.

TO THAT

Truly venerable, and excellent Character,

MR. JOHN BULL,

Whose GOOD HUMOUR is proverbial; whose
PATIENCE is *almost* unlimited; whose TASTE, in
literary matters, is not very fastidious; who loves
a good joke, though sometimes made at his own
expence; but who will never be laughed out of
his loyalty, and common sense; who, not being
able fully to comprehend the value, and profun-
dity of Modern Philosophy; but, on the contrary,
being rather prejudiced in favor of such old
fashioned things, as kingly governments and
the Bible, always looks with a suspicious eye at
unusual professions of superior patriotism, and
high pretensions to new lights, and extraordinary
discoveries in Moral and Political Science,

THIS JEU D'ESPRIT,

Is most respectfully Inscribed by his sincere Friend,

THE AUTHOR OF THE

CONSTITUTIONAL HOUSE THAT JACK BUILT.

Paternoster Row, Feb. 1820.

This Day is published, in 8vo. price 5s. boards,

EVERY MAN HIS OWN
STOCK=BROKER;

OB, A COMPLETE

GUIDE TO THE PUBLIC FUNDS:

WITH THE MANNER OF

TRANSFERRING STOCK;

RULES

For Calculating the Value of any Quantity of Stock Bought or Sold, at any time; the Value of Life Annuities; the Rate of Interest; the Amount of Half-yearly Dividends; the Interest and Cost of Exchequer Bills, India Bonds, Omnium, &c.

TO WHICH ARE ADDED,

RULES

FOR STANDARDING GOLD AND SILVER COINS AND BULLION, AND FOR CALCULATING ITS VALUE.

WITH

EXTENSIVE TABLES

OF THE VALUE, WEIGHT, AND FINENESS OF THE PRINCIPAL GOLD AND SILVER COINS OF ALL THE COUNTRIES IN

EUROPE, AMERICA, &c.

———

By GEO. G. CAREY,

AUTHOR OF "A COMPLETE SYSTEM OF COMMERCIAL ARITHMETIC," &c.

LOYAL MAN IN THE MOON.

I DREAM'D one night, as some have dream'd
    before,
That I unto the Moon aloft did soar;
Reclining in a splendid air-balloon,
Made by *Lunardi*,—suited to the Moon;

B

And, as I glided through the liquid sky,
Bidding my native earth and seas " good bye,"
I felt a strange sensation in my brain,
A something which I cannot well explain—
A kind of go-between, great pleasure and
    great pain :
Though much delighted at my elevation,
Still somewhat doubtful of my situation ;
Half wishing that Old Nick had all balloons,
Or I had never known such things as Moons.
So felt the " Talents," I can well conceive,
When they had so slyly crept up George's
    sleeve,
And so Fitzwilliam, at the Yorkshire meeting,
Rejoic'd, but trembl'd, at the rabble greeting.

  Now, having pass'd the boundaries of this
    world,
Through fields of ether I was toss'd and hurl'd,
Losing all sense of space—of high or low,
Whether I rose or fell, I did not know ;
But, looking tow'rds the foot of the balloon,
To my astonishment, I saw the Moon ;
Her silvery brightness rapidly decaying ;
And a more earthy aspect fast displaying,
When soon, my mundane gas being quite
    exhausted,
My ears by human voices were accosted ;
And I was landed in a spacious town,
Just such as London—busy over grown ;

Lunan, the capital of *Luna,* it was nam'd ;
For wealth and greatness through the Moon
      'twas fam'd.
Let this suffice :—'twere useless to repeat
The name of every *Lunatarian* street.

    Finding myself, as 'twere, almost at home,
Through this vast city I began to roam,
To see the sights, as we are wont to do,
Whene'er we visit any place that's new ;
And what I there beheld, the Muse shall tell,
That after ages they may know full well,
How, in strange dreams, and visions of the
      night,
Great deeds are very often brought to light,
And truths of vast importance are reveal'd,
Which else for ever might have lain conceal'd.

    Now, in my dream I saw—or thought I saw—
Some massy volumes of MOONARIAN LAW,
In which I very plainly could perceive,
That true Lunarians had no cause to grieve
The want of good and wholesome regulations;
Such as are found in all enlighten'd nations :
In short, I thought that some Lunarian sage
From our own statute-books had stol'n a page,
The laws of Cynthia were so like our own,
One from the other scarcely could be known.

But (oh ! the great extent of vice!) I soon
Found out that *Radicals* were in the Moon!
Republicans, and Whigs, and staunch Re-
    formers;
Blasphemers, infidels, and other stormers
Of every venerable institution,
And all that's good in any constitution :
Nor was it long ere I'd an opportunity
To witness the exploits of this community :
For, very shortly after my arrival,
There happen'd in the Moon a great revival
Of what they call the spirit of reform;
In other words, a signal for a storm.
Some five or six Lunarians, very zealous,
And of their popularity most jealous,
Resolv'd that something valiant should be
    done,
Such as had ne'er been seen beneath the sun;
And so they met one very dreary night,
When this our earth had hid her brilliant light
From all Moonarian objects, to determine,
How to destroy those Lunatarian " VERMIN,"
The ministers of justice and of truth ;—
Those foes to aged vice, and friends of youth,
Who daily watch'd the disaffected tricks
Of certain crack-brain'd crazy lunatics ;
And would not very quietly submit
To lose their heads, or have their pockets
    pick'd.

Accordingly, these Moonites, full of rancour,
Met in a house, just like the

CROWN AND ANCHOR;

And there it was resolv'd, by this committee,
To hold a meeting, somewhere in the city,
To which all sorts of folks should be invited,
To see, as they declar'd, "the people righted;"
And therefore they did draw up an advertise-
     ment,
Which to the various papers straight was sent :—

I read it in *The Moonshine*, " *Leading Journal*,"
Whose publication was, they said, diurnal :
And thus it ran :————

" To every boy and every man,
Who feels himself at all aggriev'd,
And from all cares would be reliev'd,
    Thus be it known,
    To all the town,
That there will be a meeting soon
Of all the
     PEOPLE IN THE MOON:

That is, Sir Frank, and all who choose
To lick the dust from off his shoes ;

And this committee
      recommend
Every man to bring
      his friend ;
A stone, a bludgeon and
      a brick-bat ;
Resolv'd no moonly
      thing to stick at,
That should be
      needful to complete
The revolutionary
      feat ;
And there will also be
      subscriptions,
To pay for banners and
      inscriptions ;
To purchase rotten eggs
      and bones,
And fee great H——t and
      John G —— J—nes ;
And for this purpose
      open books
Are lying now with
      Mister Br——kes."

No sooner had this news gain'd circulation,
Than I observed a bustle in the nation ;
And, at the time appointed, there were seen,
Men, aye, and women too, with ardour keen,

FAST FLOCKING TO THE RENDEZVOUS,
                          with faces,
  Partaking very little of the graces;
  But full of wroth and fury; hot with rage,
  And eager in the combat to engage.
  " Gods! what a sight! what countless crowds
       were there!
  What yells, and groans, and hootings rent the
       air!"
  Oh! for great Hogarth's pencil to portray
  The motley scenes of that important day!

O that I could, the wondrous tale rehearse,
As it deserves, in pure Miltonian verse !

But not to me such lofty powers belong ;
Content if some plain moral mark my song,
And I can soothe one hour of melancholy,
Whilst answering fools according to their folly ;
More pleas'd to lash a wild licentiousness,
With its own weapon, an unbridl'd press,
Than by imprisonment, and fine, and sharp
     distress.

  Now, mark the order of this great procession,
And let it make a permanent impression.
  First march'd a monstrous mass of
       MOONY WHIGS,

c

With heads like monkies, and with tails like pigs;
Tapering, and very dandy-like in face;
But with a " broad" and most capacious base.
In every countenance was plainly seen,
A restless ardour, mix'd with much chagrin—
Puff'd up with self-conceit, pride and ambition,
Their favourite principle was *opposition*;
And as they onward walk'd, they fix'd their faces,
On certain fleeting things which they call'd places,
Pensions, and *patronage* and *sinecures*,
And whatsoever else the mind allures;
Yet, with a zeal approaching to insanity,
They loudly call'd all moonly honours vanity.
Fast on the heels of this unsightly groupe,
Came a most whimsical and motley troop
Of   **WESTERN PATRIOTS,**

full of indignation,
And vowing vengeance to the Cynthian nation.
Like some dark cloud, prophetic of a storm,
Boldly they marched in military form,
And at each step exclaim'd " Reform ! Reform !
    Reform !"
High in a curious car their leader sate,
Waving to those around his patriot hat,
Whilst some, obsequious, hanging on his skirt,
Plung'd without shame thro' every kind of dirt,
Others, as careless of their reputation,
Drew him along to their own degradation:
" All hail! Sir Frank !" the slavish rabble cried;
" All hail ! bright *Cynthia's* hope, and *Lunan's* pride !"
Next came THE RADICALS,

a hideous race,
Form'd of whate'er is impious, vile, and base ;
For, on a time the FIEND OF DISCORD
    rose,
And grasping his most huge carbuncl'd nose,
Gave a convulsive sneeze, whence quickly flew,
This host of demons—hell's infuriate crew ;
Yet these, too, boasted of " *reform*," and
    swore,
That all they sought was bread to feed the poor.
Now, reader, note this portion of my dream,
Nor blame me if I dwell upon the theme :
First comes " a monster of such frightful mien,
" That to be hated needs but to be seen."
Much like a HAMPSHIRE HOG the wretch
    appears ;
But with a scorpion's tail and ass's ears,
Mark his designing look, and cunning air,
And see if aught but knavery is there.
Sporting with sin and death, the impious elf
Carries the corpse of one just like himself ;
False and deceitful, blasphemous and base ;
Ingenious ; but of genius the disgrace.

    Close by the side of this unseemly wight
There walk'd another of these imps of night ;
With form erect, and most audacious front,
Not very much unlike our Mister H—t,
And he, too, was AN ORATOR, and wore,
A hat of dingy white, and fiercely swore,

Though, at the meeting, he should neither
    speak
Hebrew nor Latin, " *Algebra*" nor Greek,
He'd tell the boroughmongering dogs a tale
All about massacres, that should not fail
To make them " curse their stars," and sadly
    " weep and wail."
Methought this radical a bag did bear,
Of which he seem'd to take peculiar care;
And ever and anon he drew from thence
Small bits of metal, something like our pence,
It had a label bearing this inscription:
" THE WEEKLY PENNY RADICAL SUBSCRIPTION."

    Bending beneath the weight of many a year,
In this procession there did next appear,
A poor, decrepid, feeble, worn-out man,
' Whose days were dwindled to the shortest span,'
Dragging, with pain his crazy frame along,
Still, to himself, he humm'd this doleful song :

" Ye natives of this moonly ball
    Shut up your shops, and now draw near,
Tag-rag and bob-tail, whigs and all,
    Now to my ditty lend an ear :

" All things are topsy turvey turn'd,
    And have a heavy tax on ;
And I for days of yore have mourn'd ;
    For Norman, Dane, and Saxon.

" Ah! me! alas! and lack-a-day!
   No coats have our poor backs on;
For all good things are fled away
   With Norman, Dane, and Saxon.

" So now by this white hat I swear,
   And by these locks of flaxen,
For no reform will I declare,
   That is not downright Saxon."

I marvell'd much at this uncommon case,
To hear such words in so remote a place,
And I did think, that any sum I'd wager,
That they proceeded from a certain
                    MAJOR,

Whom I on earth had known full many a day,
In strains like these to pass his time away ;
Abhorring all that other men approve,
And loving only what they ceas'd to love.
Yet this strange taste — all satire now apart,—
Proceeded from the head and not the heart :
Whilst he, inspir'd with pure quixotic zeal,
For mere imaginary wrongs would feel,
And go stark staring mad—-all for the public weal.

These notes had scarcely died upon my car,
Ere I observed a frightful band appear
In this Procession, bringing up the rear.
In dirty blankets, some were warmly dress'd,
In dirtier rags and tatters were the rest,
And at the head of this unseemly tribe
Came one whom they denominated scribe,
A vile BLACK DWARF

was he, with glaring eyes
Envious and jealous,
              menacing the skies,
In a gall bladder he would
              dip his pen,
And I could hear him mutter,
              now and then,
Something about the bloody
              " Rights of Men."

Now, in my dream methought I felt the
       ground,
Trembling beneath my feet, whilst all around,
Did shrink with horror from some hideous sight:
When, lo! emerging from the shades of night,
A wretch appear'd, who bore the sacred Cross,
Heaven's glorious triumph—Hell's eternal loss—
Yet not in honour was this emblem borne,
But in derision and most impious scorn.
Now, mark the fall of all who dare to scoff
At holy things, by holy things cut off:
For in my dream methought this wretch I saw
Borne down, and crush'd beneath that very
       law,
Which cherishes, when kept—oppos'd destroys;
The source of endless pains, or endless joys.

At length, assembl'd at

THE PLACE OF MEETING.

And having pass'd the customary greeting,
Of " how do ye do?" " how are ye?" and,
   " what news?"
A President, or Chairman, they did choose ;
Which done, they rent the very air and skies,
With every species of infernal noise,
That either men or demons could devise.
When thus the worthy Chairman spoke :—
  " Order! order ! Gentlefolk ;
  I'm come to tell you wondrous things,
  All about Magistrates and Kings ;
  And to pass a Resolution,
  For the speedy Dissolution

D

127

Of the present Parliament,
That other members may be sent,
Better suited to the ends,
Of " the Prince's early Friends."
Ye People of this Cynthian nation,
Oppress'd with debt and with taxation ;
'Tis clear as mud, you never can
Be reliev'd, but on this plan :

 " First, be persuaded, that all Kings
Are most expensive useless things ;
Next, kick the Princes out of doors,
And call the nobles " sons of w—res ;"
Call every honest priest a parson,
Supported but to keep a farce on ;
Except, indeed, our good friend H———n,
Whose merits are beyond comparison ;
Because he worships us and ours,
And rails against the " higher powers."
Say, like Tom P—ne, that all Religion
Is but " a lie about a pigeon."
Call moral precepts vile restraints,
Once well enough for holy saints ;
But now completely out of season,
In this enlighten'd *Age of Reason.*
Turn every Lesson of the School
To Parody and Ridicule,
And, when convicted of a libel,
And laughing at the Holy Bible,
Then bid all decency good bye,
And give the Judge himself the lie ;

Then go to prison, breathing fury
Against the conscientious jury.
But should you chance to be acquitted,
Or those against you be out-witted,
Then call on all your friends and neighbours,
To pay you for your public labours;
And send fresh libels through the nation,
In many a dirty publication.
Fill all the Moon with puffing tales,
About the largeness of your sales;
Feeding the spirit of sedition,
In a forty-third edition,
And then, my worthy gentlefolk,
Swear 'twas a nursery tale and joke."

Thus spoke this Patriot, when I heard a yell
Of course applause, burst forth as if all hell
Had broken loose; and fiends and demons were,
Riding triumphant through the poisoned air.

And now, another of these Moonites rose,
His reformation nostrum to propose,
And thus, devoid of shame or hesitation,
Commenc'd the following singular oration:
    " Gentlemen—no, that won't do,
    I scorn to say what is not true:
    We are not gentlemen, you know,
    Then why should people call us so?
Dame Nature made us *men*, and that's enough,
And all the rest is balderdash and stuff,
        But that's no matter,
        I cannot flatter,

So listen to me, boys, I'll tell a story,
That shall promote your good and my own
    glory.
    You want reform, good neighbours, do ye?
    Then leave off drinking Gin and Noyeau,
    Rum, Brandy, Coffee, Wine and Tea,
    And what you save, why, give to me :
    I want, just now, FIVE THOUSAND POUNDS;
    And I will have it, too, or, zounds,
    I swear, I swear, by Tom Paine's grave,
    No reformation shall you have ;
    But if you willingly comply,
    And never ask a reason why,
    You may, my worthy friends, depend on't,
    I'll very quickly make an end on't.
You know my hatred to all men of quality,
And have observed my strict impartiality ;
How I have bless'd those I had curs'd before,
And often prayed, where I had oftener swore.
Then, come, and place unbounded confidence
In my integrity and common sense.
I'm just arrived from t'other side the Moon,
To punish with my pen each vile poltroon,
That dares oppose me : be he who he will,
Or king or priest, he falls before my quill.
And now, if you appreciate my merit,
And are, as I suppose, all men of spirit,
You'll see the soundness of my proposition,
To save our country from its sad condition ;
Then join together, like a mighty host,
And all subscribe to *C—b—tt's Evening Post.*"

Imagine, reader, twice ten thousand devils,
Holding in Pandæmonium their revels;
Call every frightful picture to thy view,
That Dante or great Milton ever drew;
To these Quevedo's hellish visions add,
And altogether were not half so bad,
As that which my perturb'd imagination
Depicted of the strange association,
Of every sort of uproar, yell and screech,
That followed this Reformer's daring speech.
Indeed, this meeting very much resembled,
Those held on earth, when Radicals assembled
Ere the new acts had passed to curb their
        measures,
And guard from plundering knaves, the nation's
        treasures.
Unmov'd amid this dire tremendous storm,
Stood this audacious champion of Reform,
Still urging his request with brazen face,
Unmindful of all scandal and disgrace;
Anxious alone to gain his selfish ends,
Though he should sacrifice his warmest friends.

Now, after some more noise and speechifying,
With several curious specimens of lying,
Of murders, massacres, debts, and taxation;
Of falling trade; of hunger and starvation;
Methought the scene was very quickly chang'd,
And I beheld the various speakers rang'd
Around the festive board, eating and drinking,
Nor longer of the poor, caring or thinking.

And soon drew near the genial hour for
    treason,
When potent wine usurp'd the throne of reason;
Prudence herself forgotten or despis'd,
The most romantic projects were devis'd ;
Schemes, full of contradiction and deceit,
Such as must their own wicked ends defeat,
By one or other were proposed ; but yet
Still upon one infernal object set,
All clearly tending tow'rds the vile attempt,
To bring all human laws into contempt.
In a " Black Book" a thousand names were
    written,
Marked in the day of vengeance to be smitten,
With the keen edge of some rebellious sword,
Whenever the usurper gave the word.
Libellous caricatures adorn'd the walls;
And greasy pamphlets lay on dirty stalls.
By bumpers, three times three, in quick suc-
    cession,
The President soon lost all self-possession;
And, falling from his chair, he snoring lay,
Whilst most of his supporters slunk away ;
Leaving a poor old man the shot to pay,
For which, as afterwards methought, I saw
The wretched creature, seized by force of law,
Thrown into JAIL, unheeded and forgot,
There by his faithless comrades left to rot.
Unhappy man !--his groans so loud and deep,
Entered my soul, and woke me from my sleep !

No : 'twas not dreams awoke me, 'twas the bell
Tolling my aged King's funereal knell ;
Great GEORGE, belov'd, rever'd by all the
      land,

On whom affliction laid so heavy a hand,
At length to his eternal rest is flown,
To change an earthly for a heavenly crown.
Tho' pleas'd to know he lives beyond the skies,
Well may we mourn when such a monarch dies !
Scarcely on earth so good a king now lives,
For Providence such blessings rarely gives
To sinful nations, whose ingratitude,
But ill appreciates so great a good.

    And now, ye scoffers, will ye still maintain
Your spirit of libel through another reign ?

And will ye, for some vile, ignoble bribe,
Your *present* King as heretofore describe?
Well: should you still presume to think it right,
To hold him up in every odious light,
Which your imagination can exhibit,
And you escape the prison or the gibbet,
An answer find in your licentiousness,
To all your cries about a fetter'd press.
Then, from your vile scurrility refrain,
Or cease of loss of freedom to complain;
Henceforth reserve your satire and your wit,
For those who *curse*, or those who *worship*
PITT;

Who think on *him alone* " heaven's spirit fell;"
Or deem him but the " instrument of hell."
Yes; satirize as ye will such wild extremes;
And let not thrones and altars be your themes;
But cease to scorn the law's uplifted rod:
Who honours not his KING, fears not his GOD.

THE END.

W. Shackell, Printer, Johnson's-court, Fleet-street, London.

THE

POLITICAL "*A*, APPLE-PIE;"

OR, THE

"EXTRAORDINARY RED BOOK"

VERSIFIED;

FOR THE INSTRUCTION AND AMUSEMENT OF THE RISING
GENERATION.

BY THE AUTHOR OF

"THE HOUSE THAT JACK BUILT."

𝕎𝕚𝕥𝕙 𝕋𝕨𝕖𝕟𝕥𝕪=𝕋𝕙𝕣𝕖𝕖 ℂ𝕦𝕥𝕤.

" When shall we three meet again ?"   SHAKSPEARE.

The Eighth Edition.

London:

Printed for the Author;
AND SOLD BY J. JOHNSTON, NO. 97, CHEAPSIDE.
1820.
Price One Shilling.

Should any of the Royal, Noble, Right Reverend, Right Honourable, Honourable, and most worthy Ladies and Gentlemen, described as Guests at this National Feast, imagine that they are not perfectly welcome to all the good things set before them, as far at least as the Author is concerned, they will form a very erroneous idea of the real views and feelings of him who has invited the Public to this entertainment.

*** The Reader is requested to observe, that those persons whom the Artist has chosen to place at the head of the table, have their respective names printed in Capitals, in the lines following the several Cuts ; and should there be any errors, as doubtless there may be some, in the amount of the sums, it ought in fairness to be placed to the account of the book he has versified, rather than to the Author himself. It should also be observed, that the sums total, are all exclusive of the Irish Pensions

A Owen. Printer, Doctors' Commons, London.

𝔓𝔬𝔩𝔦𝔱𝔦𝔠𝔞𝔩 𝔄, 𝔄𝔭𝔭𝔩𝔢-𝔓𝔦𝔢,

&c.

ARDEN, Lord, Register of the High Court of Admiralty; also Register of the High Court of Appeals for Prizes; likewise Register of the High Court of Delegates; is said to receive £38,574 per annum.

The *A's* altogether take about £104,484 16s. 10d.

A—APPLE PIE,

a political PIE,
To the taste quite delightful, and nice to the eye:
'Tis the PIE of the State, made of all that is good;
The ingredients all purchased by John Bull's blood:
It is bigger and better than e'er you heard mention;
Yes, bigger, by far, than LORD ARDEN's big pension.

BARRINGTON, Hon. SHUTE, Lord Bishop of Durham, £19,000.
BATHURST, Earl of, Secretary at War. and Teller of the Exchequer, &c.
receives, it is said, £32,700. The Hon. APSLEY BATHURST, one of
the Clerks along with the Earl, of the Crown Court of Chancery, also Clerk
of the Dispensations, participates in the above salary or pension. HENRY
BATHURST, Bishop of Norwich, £6,000.

The B's altogether take about £212,697 5s. 11d.

B—BIT IT,

as if he had ne'er bit before,
Though, from *Bute* down to *Burke*, 't had been bit
by a score.
The BISHOPS, God bless them, and bless all their
wigs!
They bit at this Pie, like as many fat pigs;
Though the bites that they made they were none of
them small,
Great *Barrington*'s greatly exceeded them all.
The *Bathursts* they bit a piece large as one's fist;
Brougham, Bennett, and *Burdett,* bit at it, but miss'd.

CANNING, the Hon. GEORGE, President of the Board of Trade and Controul, also Receiver-General of the Alienation Office, £6,140. STRATFORD CANNING, Minister Plenipotentiary at Switzerland, £4,276.

CASTLEREAGH, Viscount, Principal Secretary of State, and Commissioner for India Affairs, &c. £7,500.

CUMBERLAND, Duke of, Colonel of the 15th regiment of Hussars, £19,000.

CLARENCE, Duke of, Admiral of the Fleet, and Ranger of Bushy Park, £25,282.

CAMBRIDGE, Duke of, £24,000.

CATHCART, Viscount, Ambassador at St. Petersburgh, acting Minister, and Lord Vice-Admiral of Scotland, £27,364.

CROKER, Rt. Hon. J. W. First Secretary to the Admiralty, and Secretary to the Widows' Pension, £3,250. In the time of war £1,000 additional.

The C's altogether take about £362,709 14s. 5d.

C—CUT IT,

and carv'd it, and carp'd at it too,
When *Canning* and *Castlereagh* cut it in two ;
Who, born of the same fond political mother,
Whilst cutting this Pie, made a cut at each other.
The good Duke of CUMBERLAND having some
    qualms,
Soon after he married the Princess of *Salms*,

Lest enough of this Pie for himself and his wife,
He should not possess, to support them through life,
Begg'd hard for some more, and it would have been
      so,
Had not COCHRANE stepp'd in, just in time to say
      " No !"
Then *Clarence*, the Admiral, the Duke and the Ranger,
Who dismiss'd Mrs. *Jordan*, and married a stranger ;
And *Cambridge*, his brother, who married Miss *Hesse*,
Both cut pretty deeply this Apple-Pie mess.
But *Camden*, who long had enjoyed this rich feast,
And fearing the people would call him a beast,
If he ate any longer, most nobly desisted,
Whilst *Cathcart* and *Croker* as nobly persisted ;
But *Cobbett, Carlile*, and the rest of that squad,
Like the fox of the grapes, said 'twas nauseous and
      bad ;
And old Major *Cartwright*, he curs'd and he swore,
" He ne'er saw such cutting and carving before."

DUKE OF YORK, as Keeper of the King's Person during his Majesty's illness, £10,000 per ann.

DALLAS, Sir ROBERT, Knt. Chief Justice of the Court of Common Pleas, £3,500.

DUNDAS, Rt. Hon. W. &c. &c, &c. with Lady ELIZABETH ELEANORA, &c. receive in all about £14,519.

The D's altogether receive about £62,718 12s. 1d.

D—DIVIDED IT,

somewhat unfairly, 'tis said, }
When the DUKE took a piece full as large as his head, }
For merely attending his father's sick bed. }
Bob Dallas succeeding Sir *Vicary Gibbs*,
Stuck three thousand five hundred large cuts in his ribs;
And the famous *Dundasses*, with pretty Scotch names,
George, Davy, and *Willy*, and *Robert* and *James*,
With sweet Lady *Betty*, and one or two more,
Amounting in all to about half a score,
Into numerous large pieces divided this Pie,
Or the Red-book relates a most palpable lie.

ERSKINE, Lord, for having formerly been Lord Chancellor, £4,000.
ELDON, Lord High Chancellor, Speaker of the House of Lords, £18,000.
ELGIN, Earl of, having formerly been an Ambassador, &c. £2,000,
ELLIOTT, Hon. G. as Governor of the Mint, £300.
EXMOUTH, Lord, a pension of £2,000.
            The E's altogether receive about £81,725 5s. 3d.

E—ENVIED,

            and ate on't, and wishfully eyed it,
When ERSKINE, the broom-maker, tasted and tried it ;
But *Eldon*—good heavens !—what a piece did he eat,
'Twas as large as a wool-sack, and rather more sweet ;
But, yet, as he work'd pretty hard, he deserv'd it,
And if a bit fell, his good lady preserv'd it.
So *Elgin*, and *Elliott*, who governs the Mint,
Though some people say that there is nothing in't,
And *Exmouth*, who pull'd the proud Dey by the ears,
And rattled his guns 'gainst the walls of Algiers,
All partook of this Pie, some more and some less,
But little or more, they were all in the mess.

FORSTER, Rt. Hon. J. for having been Speaker of the Irish House of Commons, a pension of £5,000 per ann.

FRERE, Rt. Hon. J. H. a poet of no mean talents, as having been Minister, &c. at Madrid and Lisbon, a pension of £1,700.

FISHER, Dr. J. Bp. of Salisbury, and Chan. of the Ord. of the Gart. £ 1,770.

FOX, Mrs. E. B. widow of the late Rt. Hon. C. J. Fox, a pension of £1, 200.

FRAZER, HUGH, Deputy Provost Marshal in Jamaica, £1,554 ; other persons of this name, various pensions amounting to about £2,000 per ann.

FITZGERALD, Rt. Hon. W. V. a Lord of the Treasury, £1,600 ; other persons of this name, pensions amounting in all to about £1,500 per ann.

The F's receive altogether about £10,244 11 5.

F—FOUGHT FOR IT,

bravely, if talking and writing,
And eating and drinking, and sleeping, were fighting,
For *Forster* was Speaker, and *Frere* he wrote rhymes,
And *Fisher* lived well, in the midst of hard times ;
And old WIDOW FOX, like the famous *Jack Horner*,
Did eat her plumb-pudding, and sleep in the corner ;
Like the *Frasers*, *Fitzgeralds*, and many besides,
Who have nothing to do, but to fill their sleek hides,
With the fruit, and the juice, of this fam'd Apple-Pie,
Eat and drink well to-day, for to-morrow they die.

B

143

GEORGE III. Annual Income, as King, said to be about ONE MILLION.
GRENVILLE, Lord, Auditor of the Exchequer, a sinecure of £4,000.
GIFFORD, Sir ROBERT, Attorney-General, £6,000.
GOULBURN, HENRY, M. P. for West Looe, Under Secretary of State for the Colonies, £6,000.
GLOUCESTER, Duke of, and the Duchess, the Princess MARY, £28,000.
GORDON, Duke of, Keeper of the Great Seal of Scotland, £3,000.
GRAFTON, Duke of, a pension for life, and also as Seal Officer of the King's Bench and Common Pleas, £9,756.

The G's altogether receive about £133,970 5s. 8d.

G—GOT IT,

'twas given him, and well he deserv'd it ;
'Twas given him in trust, and full well he's preserv'd
        it ;
The *Stuarts* this treasure were made to disgorge,
It was granted to WILLIAM,—descended to GEORGE ;
And where is the wretch who will dare to declare,
That such honour great *George* was unworthy to bear ?

Though, since he received it, a few busy G's
Have each prey'd upon it, like maggots on cheese.
There's *Grenville*—heaven bless him ! because he's a
    Whig,
Yet, the piece that he got, it was rather too big :
I love all the Whigs, they're so simple and pure ;
But four thousand cuts off one Pie, to be sure,
For nothing at all, one can hardly endure.
There's busy BOB GIFFORD, the Attorney, 'tis said,
Put six thousand pieces each year in his head,
For which he's to quell every rumpus and rout,
And seize all the cannon that's " laying about."
But fam'd *Harry Goulburn*, M. P. for West Looe,
Got six thousand more, though he'd little to do.
The good Duke of *Gloucester*, and *Mary* his Duchess,
Got twenty-eight thousand big lumps in their clutches :
Much good may it do them ! for no one will say
But the Duke and his wife go each night to the play ;
And every one loves them, because they're so kind ;
And twenty-eight thousand *John Bull* does not mind.
Then *Gordon*, to shew that he was not asleep,
Got three thousand pieces away at a sweep,
To keep the Scotch seal—though they've got none to
    keep.
And *Grafton*, above all manœuvres and tricks,
Nine thousand seven hundred and fifty and six,
He got, and that honestly, too, I declare,
For though he's a Whig, he's a right to a share ;
But *Grattan*, and *Grosvenor*, and noble Earl *Grey*,
Thought this Pie was most wantonly given away ;
And swore such proceedings it never would do,
Unless they themselves had a finger in't too.

HASTINGS, Marquis of, and Earl MOIRA, Governor-General of India, and Constable and Governor of the Tower of London, about £25,947.

HERTFORD, Marquis of, Lord Chamberlain, £3,000.

HARCOURT, Earl of, Master of the Robes and of the Horse to the Queen; for expences of Windsor Park; and as Governor of the Royal Military College; and the Countess of HARCOURT, Lady of the Queen's Bedchamber, together about £8,100.

HILL, Lord, a pension of £2,000; also as Governor of Hull, £180.

HUNN, MARY and MARIA, Mother and Sister to the Rt. Hon. G. Canning, £500.

HOLLAND, Lord, Rec.-Gen. of the issues of Glamorg. Monmouth, &c. granted to his Lordship and his Assigns, during the Lives of C. J. Fox and H. E. Fox the survivor, £350.

HUSKISSON, W. Esq, M. P. a *reversion* in case of losing office, £1,200; also as Colonial Agent for Ceylon, and Commissioner of Woods, Forests, and Land Revenues; also, ELIZA EMILY HUSKISSON, to commence on the Death of her husband, £615. In all about £2,400.

The *H*'s altogether take about £131,250 0s. 10d.

H—HAD IT—

Oh! 'twas a miraculous dish!
Unlike every other of fowl, flesh, or fish:
Whilst one man had got it, another partook on't,
And many did wish for't, who scarcely would look on't.

146

Lord *Hastings!*—my stars! was the like ever seen?
His lordship, in England, quite lanky and lean,
A few years having fed on this Pie in the East,
Grew sleeky and fat as a Staffordshire beast:
And, indeed, well he might, for 'twere monstrous
        strange,
If twenty-five thousand a year did not change
Any man upon earth, who before had but little,
Yet now has all things that just suit to a tittle.
Lord *Hertford*, the loyal, good-humour'd, and true, ⎫
Had three thousand pieces, with nothing to do, ⎬
But how much HIS LADY had nobody knew; ⎭
For, though much belov'd by the Prince of the Pie, ⎫
Her ladyship was most remarkably shy, ⎬
And took what she had, as they say, " on the sly." ⎭
The *Harcourts*, who kept the King's robes, neat and
        clean,
The horses, and bedchamber, too, of the Queen,
(Though the King being sickly, his robes never wore,
And the Queen had no horse—for the Queen was no
        more,)
Of this great Apple-Pie received many a large slice,
Which the Earl said was good, and the Countess call'd
        nice.
Lord *Hill* had a bit on't for killing the French,
So had good mother *Hunn*, and her sweet pretty wench.
The piece that was had by that notable Whig
Lord *Holland*, was not so remarkably big;
But, yet, notwithstanding the piece was so small,
'Twas a wonder a Whig should take any at all.
The *Huskissons*, thinking 'twas glorious diversion,
Had many large cuts, besides more in *reversion;*
But *Harrison, Hobhouse, Hunt, Harvey,* and *Hone,*
Being unable to get it, all let it alone.

JACKSON, Dr. WILLIAM, Lord Bishop of Oxford, £3,300.
JONES, WILLIAM, Esq. Marshal of the King's Bench Prison, a place supposed to be worth about £5,000 per ann.

The I's and J's altogether receive about £22,070 14s. 1d.

J—JOINED AT IT,

but the division was partial,
For JACKSON the Bishop,
and JONES the Bench Marshal,
Help'd themselves so profusely,
that some people said,
Scarce a bit had the others
to put in their head.

KENT, Duke of, Governor of Gibraltar, Colonel of the royal Scotch regiment of foot, and Ranger of Hampton Court Little Park, £31,205.

KENYON, Lord, and J. RICHARDSON, Custos Brev. in the King's Bench, £1,861.

KENYON, Hon. R. S. Filazer, Exigenter, &c. Court of King's Bench, £4,986.

KING, Dr. WALTER, Bp. of Rochester, &c. &c. £5,400.

The K's altogether take about £77,798 15s. 3d.

K—KEPT IT,

perhaps merely out of a whim,
For, somehow or other, it would not keep him;
For though royal KENT ate enough for a score,
He grew very thin, and still wanted some more.
His lordship of Rochester, good *Walter King*,
Kept a bit for himself, though he call'd it a *thing*,
And loath'd and despis'd it, as feeling his mind
Was set upon things of a different kind;
His lordship so much upon holy things thinking,
He scarce gave a thought about eating or drinking.
But not so some others :— the *Kenyons*, to wit,
They lik'd all they kept, and that was not a bit.

LAKE, Viscount, Lord of the Bedchamber, £13,649.

LAW, JOHN, D.D. Bishop of Elphin, £5,500.

LAW, GEORGE HENRY, Lord Bishop of Chester, &c. £3,900,

LIVERPOOL, Earl of, Constable of Dover Castle, First Lord of the Treasury, Commissioner for the Affairs of India, and Clerk of the Pells in Ireland, £13,100.

LONG, Right Hon. C. M. P. for Haslemere, Paymaster of the Forces, £3,500.

LOWTHER, Viscount, M. P. for Westmoreland, Commissioner for Affairs o India, and Lord of the Treasury, £3,100.

The *L*'s altogether receive about £55,763 3s.

L—LONG'D FOR IT,

like a child longing for cake,
Nor long'd he in vain, for the noble Lord *Lake*
Got a piece by his longing as large as a church,
Though others who long'd for't were left in the lurch.
Lord LIVERPOOL, also, was seized with the fit;
Law, Lowther, and *Long,* likewise, wish'd for a bit;
And their wishes were shortly most amply supplied,
For they ate so much of it, some thought they'd have
died.

MONTAGUE, MAT. Duke of Manchester, Captain-General and Governor of Jamaica, £15,000.

MANSELL, WILLIAD LORT, Bishop of Bristol, £3,200,

MANSFIELD, Countess of, Deputy Ranger of Richmond Park, £1,600.

MARCH, CHARLES, late Principal Clerk of the War Office, £1,000.

MARKHAM, OSBORN, and F. LE BLANC, Clerks of the King's Bench, £8,391.

MARLBOROUGH, Duke of, pension, £5,000,

MARSH, HERBERT, D. D. Lord Bishop of Llandaff, £1,400.

MELVILLE, ROBERT, Viscount, First Lord of the Admiralty, £5,000, Viscountess, Lady of the Queen's Bedchamber, £500,

MITFORD, R. Agent for the Scotch Exchequer in England, £2,000,

MONTFORD, Lord, £800.

MONTROSE, Duke of, Master of the Horse, and Lord Justice-General of Scotland, £3,266 13s, 4d.

MOORE, Rev. G. C. and Reverend R, Registrars Prerogative Court, £3,670.

MACDONALD, Sir A. [now dead] pensions, £3,300.

MALMESBURY, Earl of, £2,300.

MORRISON, T. Receiver of Fees and Emoluments in the office of the Mint in the Tower, £2,753.

The M's altogether take about £144,873 17s. 7d.

M—MOURN'D FOR IT,

and a strange mourning was there,
Some smil'd whilst they mourn'd,
and some mourn'd in despair ;

C

As the Conqueror, who,
          having the world overrun,
Did weep that another
          world could not be won,
So lamented these men
          at this glorious repast,
And ceas'd not to gormandize
          whilst it would last.
Of the weeping philosophers
          few had less cause
To complain of his share,
          than the Duke of *Montrose;*
Nor had *Mansell* much reason
          to weep and lament,
Though his office it taught him
          to sigh and repent.
The COUNTESS of MANSFIELD might laugh
    whilst she wept,
For full sixteen hundred large pieces she kept;
And all that she did for't was ranging the Park
Or capering at puppet shows, gay as a lark.
But *Marlborough,* I grant, he might grumble a bit,
For with five thousand pounds he was poor as a nit;
Though on much less than this did grow fat the Lord
    Montfort;
But his Grace was a book-worm, and that may ac-
    count for't.
Bob Mitford, and *Markham, Macdonald,* and *March,*
And *Malmesbury* and *Montague, Melville* and *Marsh,*
With the *Morrisons, Moores,* aye, and many besides,
All laugh'd till they cried, as if splitting their sides.

NORTH, Hon. BROWNLOW, Bishop of Winchester, £12,000.
NORTHINGTONS, The, Sisters and Co-heiresses of the Earl of, £2,070
NORTON, FLETCHER, Baron of Exchequer, £2,865 10s· 5d.
NEVILLE, H. Earl of Abergavenny—office abolished.
NELSON, Lord, his survivors receive, it is said, £9,700.
NEWCASTLE, Duchess Dowager, £1,000.
NICHOLL, Sir JOHN, official Principal of the Court of Arches, £5,000.
        The N's altogether take about £50,444 8s. 8d.

N—NODDED,

                and wink'd, and look'd wonderful sly,
When first he beheld this miraculous Pie.
The *Northingtons,* bless their delightful sweet faces !
They nodded assent, as they sat in their places ;
Whilst they ate of this Pie, with great relish and taste,
NORTON pick'd up the crumbs, that there might be
        no waste.
The Patent Inspector, the great *Harry Neville,*
He nodded adieu, and look'd black as the Devil ;
But *Nelson,* who whipp'd the proud French with a rod,
Taught his friends how to make a most elegant nod.
North, Nicholl, Newcastle, and two or three more,
All nodded to sleep, and fell flat on the floor.

OAKES Sir HILDIBRAND, Lieutenant-General of the Ordnance, £1,559.
ONSLOW, A. and his Son, G. ONSLOW, and the longest liver, £3,000.
OUSELEY, Sir GORE, Ambassador in Persia, £5,102 5s.

The O's altogether take about £21,263 4s. 3d.

O—OPEN'D IT,

gently,—'twas one of his jokes,
When Lieutenant-General
Sir *Hildibrand* OAKES,
Made a dash at the in-meat,
nor miss'd he his aim,
For he seiz'd so much of it,
the rest cried " For shame !"
But *Onslow* and *Ouseley*
they both did the same.

PRINCE REGENT, Prince of Wales, D. of Cornwall, &c. &c. sum unknown.
PARSONS, J. Bishop of Peterborough, £2,300.
PELHAM, Hon. GEORGE, Bishop of Exeter, £3,900
PERCEVAL, Hon. JANE, (now CARR) pension, £2,000.
PERCEVAL, SPENCER, Teller of the Exchequer, £2,700.
PLAT, S. and J. Clerks of the Papers, £2675.
PLUMER, Sir T. Master of the Rolls, £4,000.
POLE, W. W. Right Hon. Master of the Mint, £13,000.
POWYS, E. Dean of Canterbury, £1,000.

The P's altogether take about £78,916 10s. 2d.

P—PEEP'D INTO'T,

eagerly poring and prying,
Like Coventry Tom the fair lady espying:
Tom paid for his peeping, by losing his eye,
And so have some others, who peep'd at this Pie:
For what foreign foe e'er presum'd to peep here,
Whom we did not send back with a flea in his ear?

But, Oh ! had you seen the significant glance,
When the PRINCE so delightfully looking askance,
Most graciously cast his own fine royal eye,
At the fruit and the crust of this great Apple-Pie !
No eye ever look'd with more ardour or grace,
Or love more intensely e'er gaz'd on a face :
Oh, yes, though a leer, it was full of desire :—
Though merely a peep it was pregnant with fire.
The *Priests*, though abstracted from worldly affairs,
On things more substantial bestowing their cares,
They could not but feel, as they gravely pass'd by,
There was something more tempting in this Apple-Pie·
Hence *Pelham* and *Parsons*, and one or two more,
Put their hands to the fruit, like their daddy of yore.
My stars ! what a look gave the good *Wellesley Pole !*
In his eye you might plainly perceive all his soul ;
Nor could *Plumer* or *Perceval*, *Powys* or *Plat*,
Be said to look heedlessly, foolish, or flat,
As peeping, and pointing, and passing along,
They humm'd to themselves this fag end of a song :
" We see in this Pie all that's lovely and comely,
" And home it is home, be it ever so homely."
Now, amongst all the persons who peep'd at this Pie,
A strange motley group, call'd " The People,"
        pass'd by ;
But presuming to ask for a peep and a bite,
Got a kick o' their bottoms, which serv'd them just
        right ;
For 'twas properly ask'd, " What have *Peasants* to do
" With a Pie, but to work hard, that others may
        chew ?"

QUARME, R. G. Usher of the Black Rod, House of Peers, £2,000.
QUARME, R. Gentleman Usher of the Green Rod to the Order of the Thistle, £100.

The Q's together take about £2,100.

Q—QUARTER'D IT,

thinking it could do us no harm,
And a portion was given to
GEORGE and BOB QUARME;
But the manner in which they
devour'd it was odd,
For they pok'd out the fruit
with a black and green rod.

RICHMOND, Duke of, £12,666 13s. 4d,
ROBINSON, Right Hon. F. J. M. P. for Rippon, Treasury of the Navy, £3,000.—ROBINSON, Sir F. P. Governor of Tobago, £1,500.
ROSE, W. S. Clerk of the Exchequer of Pleas, M. P. for Tiverton, £2,137.—
ROSE B. H. Ambassador at Berlin, £6,677 9s. 7d.
RYDER, Hon. H. Bishop of Gloucester, £2,103.

The *R*'s altogether take about £78,135 5s. 5d.

R—RAN FOR IT—

oh, 'twas a capital race !
Some ran for a pension, and some for a place ;
But, running too fast, many met with a fall,
And *Richmond* considerably distanc'd them all.
The *Roses*, however, came in, in fine style,
With the *Robinsons* following them scarcely a mile.
Alas ! for his lordship, the great Bishop RYDER,
He said, that unless they would make the course wider,
He never could drag his fat carcass along,
The racers they were such a terrible throng.
And as for *Reformers*, still run as they wou'd,
Their running or walking would do them no good.
The *Radicals* run themselves quite out of breath,
And bouncing about they fell flat on the earth ;
Then rending the air with this horrible cry :
" Oh give us some bread, for we've none of the Pie !"

SALISBURY, Marquis of, Joint Post-Master-General with the Earl of CHI-CHESTER, £2,500.

SCOTT, Right Hon. Sir W. M P. for Oxford University, Judge of the Consistory Court, and Judge of the Admiralty Court, £6,694.

SCOTT, WALTER, Sheriff Depute for the shire of Selkirk, and Clerk of the Court of Session, £3,590.

SEYMOUR, Lords R. and H. brothers, both fill one office, viz. Prothonotary in the Court of King's Bench, in Ireland, £6,849.

SHAFTESBURY, Earl, Chairman of Commit. to the House of Lords, £2,661.

SIDMOUTH, Viscount, Secretary of State for the Home Department, and Commissioner for the Affairs of India, £7,500.

SMITH, Sir W. SIDNEY, £2,000.

SOPHIA, P incess, £7,000.— SOPHIA AUGUSTA, Princess £9,000.— SOPHIA OF GLOUCESTER, Princess, £9,000.

SOUTHEY, ROBERT, Poet Laureat, £100 ; 31st March, 1807, £200.

SPARKE, B. E. Bishop of Ely, £5,500.

STEWART, Lord, Ambassador to the Court of Vienna, Lord of the Bedchamber, and Col. of the 25th dragoons, £15,700.

SUSSEX, Duke of, £18,000.

SUTTON, C. M. Speaker of the House of Commons, £6,000.

SUTTON, C. M. Archbishop of Canterbury, £28,000.

The S's altogether take about £254,608 7s. 8d.

S—SIGH'D FOR'T,

and sought it, and sung for it too,
Still keeping the same tempting object in view.

D

159

O ! there was such seeking,
           and singing, and sighing,
And " trembling, and hoping,
           and lingering, and flying,"
All bending their steps to
           this one point of meeting,
As if their salvation
           depended on eating !
The Princess SOPHIA—
           AUGUSTA, her sister,
And their royal relation,
           SOPHIA of Gloster,
In concert sent forth
           a most languishing sigh,
At twenty-five thousand
           large cuts off this Pie.
Bob Southey, who sung in the praise of Wat Tyler,
And once of this Pie a most sturdy reviler,
Having suddenly changed his melifluous strains,
Got some pounds every year of the same for his pains :
But scarce had his bardship sat down to his meal,
Ere a terrible stupor beginning to feel,
Gave evidence clear as the sun in the sky,
That no poet sings well, who sings merely for Pie.
The fam'd *Walter Scott,* his great talents to show,
Sung " Roderigh Vich Alpine ! dhu ho ieroe !"
And the sense was so plain, and the words were so pretty,
That Walter received for his wonderful ditty
As much as would fairly have fatten'd a score
Of such poets as Bloomfield, Tom Campbell, or Moore.
Great *Scott,* the wise Judge of the Admiralty Court,
Thought seeking this Pie such uncommon good sport,
That, without more ado, he soon join'd in the play,
And carried seven thousand per annum away.

But, Oh ! what deep sighs did proceed from the *Sut-*
    tons,
As they gorg'd at this feast like as many fat gluttons ;
And as persons saw an archbishop thus feeding,
(Whilst the poor at each pore were most piteously
    bleeding,)
So unlike his Great Master :—all things in possession,
They thought they saw cause to suspect his succession :
Observing a Pastor with Kings on a level,
They cried out, " Oh ! Antichrist, Pope, and the
    Devil !"
Lord *Sidmouth*, on hearing this blasphemous cry, ⎞
(His lordship replete with the fruit of this Pie,) ⎟
From the depth of his soul fetch'd a most heavy sigh, ⎠
And declar'd, if the dogs thus insulted their betters,
He'd instantly choke them with circular letters.
'Mongst these seekers, and sighers, and those who die
    daily,
I should not omit the good Bishop of Ely,
The kind, the benevolent, excellent *Sparke,*
Fam'd for preaching and praying, and hitting a mark.
Lord *Stewart*, he sigh'd to some purpose indeed,
For a piece was soon given him sufficient to feed
A hundred such men ; aye, and had he another,
He was welcome, because he was Castlereagh's brother.
Great *Sussex*, of princes the marrow and pith,
With *Salisbury* and *Shaftesbury*, *Seymour* and *Smith*,
All sigh'd with success for a piece of this Pie,
Though many who sigh'd got a kick for each sigh :
'Twas just as it should be, for ought such a mine
Be taken from Princes and cast before " *Swine ?*"

TALBOT, C. CHETWYND, Earl Lord Lieutenant of Ireland, £30,000.
TAYLOR, B. Envoy Extra. and Minister Plenipo. at Wirtemburg, £4,276.
THOMAS, NASSAU, Master of the Robes, (salaries in his department,) £800.
THORNTON, EDWARD, Ambassador and Minister Plenipotentiary at Brazils, £5,300.
THURLOW, Lord EDWARD, Clerk of the Custodies of Idiots and Lunatics, (Court of Chancery,) Office for executing the Laws concerning Bankrupts, and Clerk of the Presentations in the Court of Chancery, £6,713.
THYNNE, Lord. GEORGE, Comptroller of the King's Household, £1,200.
TOMLINE, GEORGE, Bishop of Lincoln, and Dean and Canon Residentiary of St. Paul's, £5,100.
TORRINGTON, Lord, late Minister Plenipotentiary at Brussels, £1,684.
TUCKER, B. Deputy Secretary to the Lords of the Admiralty, £1,082.
The T's altogether take about £98,239 8s. 9d.

T—TOOK IT;

but whether he toil'd for it too,
My author has hitherto kept out of view :
Be that as it may, friend T took it and kept it,
When TALBOT and THURLOW so handsomely
    swept it,
And *Thomson* and *Thornton*, and *Tomline* and *Thynne*,
All took many pieces, and thought it no sin ;
So did *Taylor* and *Torrington*, *Thomas* and *Tucker* ;
But *Tierney* he was in a terrible *pucker*,
And swore if the *Tories* they took at this rate,
They would leave poor John Bull not a morsel to eat.

VANSITTART, Right Hon. NICHOLAS, Chancellor of the Exchequer, M, P. for Harwich, Lord of the Treasury, Commissioner for the Affairs of India, and Under Treasurer of the Exchequer, £7,500.

VAUGHAN, C. Secretary of Embassy at Madrid, £1,136 10s.

VERNON, CAROLINE, Maid of Honour to the Queen, £300.

VILLIERS, Hon. GEORGE, Paymaster of Marines, and Groom of the Bed-chamber to the King, £3,300.

VIVIAN, JOHN, and E. W. CARR, Solicitors of the Excise, £15,913.

VYSE, W. Archdeacon of Coventry, and Rector of Lambeth, £1,700.

The V's and U's altogether take about £40,170 1s. 3d.

V—VIEW'D IT,

and finding it toothsome and good,
Said he liked it as much as he liked his own blood,
When the pious VANSITTART, the Treasury Lord,
That great calculator, and man of his word ;
That framer of bills about payments and cash,
Not long did stand viewing, but making a dash,
Nearly made of this Pie a mere hodge-podge and hash. }
JOHN VIVIAN, solicitor of the Excise,
The Reverend, disinterested, good *William* VYSE,
Also *Caroline* VERNON, the sweet maid of honour
To the Queen—though the Queen needs no maid to
          wait on her ;
Likewise *Villiers*, and *Vaughan*, and many *V's* more,
This Pie of the state came to view and adore.

WALES, Princess of, £35,000.

WALSINGHAM, Lord, Comptroller of First Fruits (Court of Exchequer,) also a Pension of £2,000,—£2,150.

WARD, ROBERT, M. P. for Haslemere, Clerk of the Ordnance, £1,914.

WARREN, Sir JOHN BORLASE, £2,000.

WARRENDER, Sir GEORGE, a Lord of the Admiralty, £1,500.

WELLESLEY, Right Hon. Sir HENRY, Ambassador at Madrid, £10,603,

WELLINGTON, Duke of, &c. &c. It is impossible to state the precise amount of his Grace's income, but it may be estimated on a moderate supposition at £30,000.

WESTMORLAND, J. F. Earl of, Lord of Privy Seal, £3,000.

WINCHESTER, Marquis of, Groom of the Stole, £2,000.

WYNDHAM, Hoh. P. C. Register in Chancery in Jamaica, and Secretary and Clerk of Council in Barbadoes, £2,170.

WYNNE, H. W. W. late Envoy at the Court of Dresden, £1,200.

The *W*'s recceive altogether about £130,462 2s. 2d.

W—WISH'D FOR'T,

but wishing, and wishing won't do,
Or the *Whigs* had long had it : I say what is true ;
For ,to my certain knowledge, for this Apple Pie,
They have wish'd till they almost were ready to die ;
And 'tis every where known, that to this very hour,
They are panting for places, and pensions, and power:

Well, let them wih on ; for in spite of their panting,
The Whigs, I'm Jersuaded, they still must be wanting.
Yet let not frienc *W*. wish in despair,
For, indeed, he comes in for a plentiful share.
That unfortunite exile, the *Princess of Wales*,
The subject and victim of all sorts of tales,
Some true and some false, whate'er be her wish,
Enjoys no small share of this excellent dish.
The *Marquis of Winchester*, Groom of the Stole,
Though he had not exactly the wish of his soul,
Having nothing to do for the lumps he receiv'd,
With two thousand per annum he was not much griev'd.
Great *Wellington* certainly had much to do,
In beating *Napoleon*, at fam'd *Waterloo*;
And so well has his country rewarded his skill,
Should he eat all we've given him, I'm certain it will,
If not burst him outright, make him terribly ill.
Lord *Wellesley*, *Walsingham*, *Wyndham*, and *Wynne*,
Lest wishing for Pie they should grow very thin,
Were supplied with as much as they fairly could stuff,
And yet they scarce thought they had all got enough.
So *Westmoreland*, *Warrender*, *Warren*, and *Ward*,
All seemed to conceive it was cruel and hard,
That they were not permitted to have all they wanted,
Tho', in fact, for the whole of this Pie they all panted.
Now *Wolseley* and *Wooller*, and *Waithman* and *Wood*,
Admitting the Pie to be wholesome and good,
All declared that they never had wished for a bit on't,
And just as they said so, old WATSON he spit on't;
But some persons thought that the nasty old elf,
Only did it to have the whole Pie to himself.

YORK, Duke of, Commander in Chief of his Majesty's Forces, Keeper and 'Lieutenant of his Majesty's Forest, Parks, and Warrens at Windsor, and for holding Swanimote Courts in Windsor Forest, £40,631 16s. 7d.—Also see Letter D.

YORK, Duchess of, £4,000.

YORK, Right Hon. EDW. VENABLES VERNON, Archbishop of, £12,000.

YORKE, Right Hon. C. P. Teller of the Exchequer, £2,700.

The Y's altogether take about £62,503 6s. 4d.

Y—YAWN'D O'ER IT,

weari'd with eating and drinking;
For *York* ate sufficient, at least, to my thinking,
To feed half the army, as armies are fed ;
Whilst poor old JOHN BULL, o'er the empty dish
     said,
 ʼ Ah! there's none left for me, nor for X, nor for Z."

THE END.

Owen, Printer Doctors' Commons.

THE QUEEN'S
MATRIMONIAL LADDER,

A National Toy,

WITH FOURTEEN STEP SCENES;

AND

ILLUSTRATIONS IN VERSE,

WITH EIGHTEEN OTHER CUTS.

BY THE AUTHOR OF " THE POLITICAL HOUSE THAT JACK BUILT."

" The question is not merely whether the Queen shall have her rights, but whether the rights of any individual in the kingdom shall be free from violation."

Her Majesty's Answer to the Norwich Address.

" Here is a Gentleman, and a friend of mine!"
Measure for Measure.

Twenty-first Edition.

LONDON:
PRINTED BY AND FOR WILLIAM HONE, LUDGATE-HILL.

1820.

This Pamphlet and the Toy together,
ONE SHILLING.

'It is a wonderful thing to consider the strength of Princes' wills when they are bent to have their Pleasure fulfilled, wherein no reasonable persuasions will serve their turn: how little do they regard the dangerous sequels, that may ensue as well to themselves as to their Subjects. And amongst all things there is nothing that makes them more wilful than Carnal Love, and various affecting of voluptuous desires."

Cavendish's Memoirs of Card. Wolsey.

NOTE.

All the Drawings for this Publication are

By Mr. GEORGE CRUIKSHANK.

Give not thy strength unto women, nor thy ways to that which destroyeth kings.

Solomon.

QUALIFICATION.

In love, and in drink, and o'ertoppled by debt;
With women, with wine, and with duns on the fret.

Penury incurr'd
By endless riot, vanity; the lust
Of pleasure and variety !———.
——————Ministerial grace
Deals him out money from the public chest.

Cowper.

DECLARATION.

The Prodigal Son, by his perils surrounded,
Vex'd, harass'd, bewilder'd, asham'd, and con-
   founded,
Fled for help to his Father,
   confessed his ill doing,
And begged for salvation
   from stark staring ruin;
The sire urged—" The People
   your debts have twice paid,
" And, to ask a third time,
   even Pitt is afraid;
" But he shall if you'll marry, and lead a new life,—
" You've a cousin in Germany—make her your
   wife!"

Lured from her own, her native home,
The home of early life,
And doom'd in stranger realms to roam;
A widow ! yet a wife !

Phillips's Lament.

ACCEPTATION.

From the high halls of Brunswick, all youthful and
  gay,
From the hearth of her fathers, he lured her away :
How joy'd she in coming—
      how smiling the bower;
How sparkling their nuptials—
      how welcome her dower.
Ah ! short were her pleasures—full soon came her
  cares—
Her husbandless bride-bed was wash'd with her
  tears.

B

The most desolate woman in the world!

Thy daughter, *then*, could hear thee weep ;
But now she sleeps the dreamless sleep.

Phillips's Lament.

ALTERATION.

Near a million of debts gone,
        all gone were her charms—
What! an Epicure have *his own* wife
        in his arms?
She was not to his *taste*—
        what car'd *he* for the ' form,'
' To love and to cherish'
        could not mean reform :
' To love' meant, of course, nothing else
        but neglect ;—
' To cherish' to leave her,
        and shew disrespect.

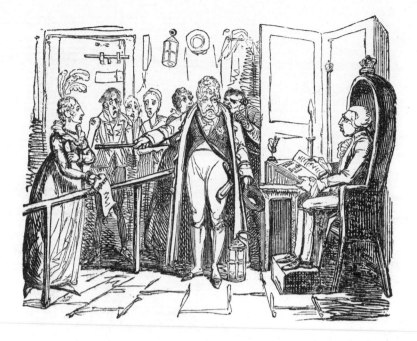

——————faded appetite resign'd
The victim up to shame.

Phillips's Lament.

IMPUTATION.

Was it manly, when widow'd,
   to spy at her actions;
To listen to eaves-droppers,
   whisp'ring detractions;
And, like an old WATCHMAN,
   with faults to conceal,
Get up a *false Charge,*
   as a proof of his zeal?
If desertion was base, Oh base be his name,
Who, having deserted, would bring her to shame

God, and your Majesty, protect mine innocence !

King Henry VIII.

EXCULPATION.

Undaunted in spirit, her courage arose,
With encrease of charges, and encrease of foes.
Despising the husband,
        who thus had abused her,
She proved to his father,
        his son had ill used her:—
Her conduct examin'd, and sifted, shone bright,
Her enemies fled, as the shadows of night.

—— A wanderer, far away,
Neglected and reviled—
Phillips's Lament.

EMIGRATION.

Her father and king, while with reason yet blest,
Protected her weakness, and shielded her rest;
Infirmity seizes him, false friends draw near,
Then spies gather round, and malignants appear;
And cajole, wait, watch, insult,
           alarm, and betray,
Till from home, and her daughter,
           they force her away.

'A hundred thousand welcomes!'

Coriolanus.

REMIGRATION.

Still pursued, when a 'wanderer,'
    her child sleeps in death,
And her best friend, in England, her king,
    yields his breath ;
This gives her new rights—
    they neglect and proscribe her ;
She threatens returning—they then try to bribe her !
The bullies turn slaves, and, in meanness, fawn on her:
They feel her contempt, and they vow her dishonour ;
But she 'steers her own course,' comes indignantly
  over,
And the shouts of the nation salute her at Dover!

He smelt—O Lord! how he did smell!
Southey's Minor Poems, vol. iii. *v.* 103.

CONSTERNATION.

Ah, what was that groan!—
      'twas the Head of the Church,
When he found she was come—
      for he dreaded a search
Into what *he*'d been doing :
      and sorely afraid, for
What *she* might find out,
      cried ' *I'll not have her pray'd for* ';
And the B——ps, obeying their *pious* Head,
      care took
That the name of his wife
      should be out of the prayer book !

———— I will kill thee, if thou dost deny
Thou hast made me a cuckold.

——————————————What false Italian
(As poisonous tongued as handed) hath prevailed
On thy too ready hearing?

Cymbeline.

ACCUSATION.

On searching for precedents, much to their dread,
They found that they could n't well cut off her head;

And the ' House of Incurables' raised a ' Report'
She was not a fit person to live in *his* Court.
How like an OLD CHARLEY
        they then made him stand,
In his lanthorn a *leech*,
        the ' Report' in his hand.
' Good folks be so good as not go near that door
' For, though my own wife, she *is*—I could say more
' But it's all in this *Bag*, and there'll be a fine pother,
' I shall get rid of her, and I'll then get another!'

  Yet he thought, to himself,—
        'twas a thought most distressing,—
' If *she* should discover
        I've been M—ch—ss—g,
' There's an end of the whole!
        D——rs C——ns, of course,
' If *my own* hands are dirty,
        won't grant a D——ce!'

He tried to look wise, but he only look'd wild;
The women laugh'd out, and the grave even smiled;
The old frown'd upon him—the children made sport,
And his wife held her *ridicule* at his ' Report'!

MORAL.

Be warn'd by his fate
Married, single, and all;
Ye elderly Gentlemen,
Pity his fall!

c

Give me but the Liberty of the Press, and I will give to the minister a venal House of Peers.   *Sheridan.*

PUBLICATION.

As yon bright orb, that vivifies our ball,
Sees through our system, and illumines all;

So, sees and shines, our MORAL SUN, THE PRESS,
Alike to vivify the mind, and bless;
Sees, the rat *Leech* turn towards Milan's walls,
' Till the black slime betrays him as he crawls;'
Sees, from that recreant, vile, and eunuch-land,
Where felon-perjurers hold their market-stand,
Cooke, with his ' cheek of parchment, eye of stone,'
Get up the evidence, to go well down;
Sees who, with eager hands, the Green Bag cram,
And warns the nation of the frightful flam ;
Sees Him, for whom they work the treacherous
        task,
With face, scarce half conceal'd, behind their mask.
Fat, fifty-eight, and frisky, still a beau,
Grasping a half-made match, by *Leech*-light go;
Led by a passion, prurient, blind, and batter'd,
Lame, bloated, pointless, flameless, age'd and
        shatter'd ;
Creeping, like Guy Fawkes, to blow up his wife,
Whom, spurn'd in youth, he dogs through after-life.

    Scorn'd, exiled, baffled, goaded in distress,
She owes her safety to a fearless Press:
With all the freedom that it makes its own,
It guards, alike, the people and their throne;
While fools with darkling eye-balls shun its gaze,
And soaring villains scorch beneath its blaze.

I am wrapp'd in dismal thinkings!—

THE KING, in *All's well that ends well.*

INDIGNATION.

The day will soon come, when ' the Judge and the
      Ponderer,'
Will judge between thee, and the charge-daring
      ' Wanderer ;'
Will say—' Thou who cast the first stone at thy wife,
Art thou without sin, and is spotless *thy* life?'
Ah! what if *thy* faults should ' outrival the sloe,'
And thy wife's, beside thine, should look ' whiter
      than snow ' !
   Bethink thee! the old British Lion awoke,
Turns indignant, and treads out thy bag-full of smoke.
Spurn thy minions—the traitors, who counsel thee,
      banish;
And the soldiers will quickly forget all their *Spanish!*

" Le Roy le veut !" G. R.

See Blackstone's Com. b. 1. c. 2.

CORONATION.

Shakspeare says, in King John, it's a curse most
     abhorrent,
That '*Slaves* take the humours of Kings for a warrant.'
A more *useful* truth never fell from his pen,
If Kings would apply it like sober-bred men.
The Slaves of *your* will,
         will make your reign, in History,
A misrule of force, folly, taxing, and mystery :
Indulging your wish for
         what, with law, 's incompatible,
For the present, they've render'd your crown
         not come-at-able ;
And the tongues of old women and infancy wag,
With, ' He call'd for his crown—and
         they gave him the *Bag !*'

So let him stand * * * * *
* * * * * * * * * * * *

Byron.

DEGRADATION.

To this have they brought thee, at last!

Exposed thee, for all men to see!
Ah, surely, their pandering
        shall quickly be past:—
‘ How wretched their portion
        shall be!
‘ Derision shall strike them
        forlorn,
    ‘ A mockery that never shall die:
‘ The curses of hate and the hisses
        of scorn,
    ·Shall follow wherever they fly;
‘ And proud o’er their ruin
        for ever be hurl’d,
    ‘ The laughter of triumph,
        the jeers of the world!’

THE END

" Cuts’ Meat!"
English Cry.

I say, HUM, how fares it with Royalty now?
Is it *up*?—Is it *prime*?—Is it *spooney*?—or how?
The Fudge Family.

THE JOSS AND HIS FOLLY,

An Extract of an overland Dispatch.

I stare at it from out my casement,
And ask for what is such a place meant.

Byron.

July 29, 1820.

——The queerest of all the queer sights
I've set sight on ;—
Is, the *what d'ye-call'-t thing*, here,
THE FOLLY at Brighton

The outside—huge teapots,
          all drill'd round with holes,
Relieved by extinguishers,
          sticking on poles:
The inside—all tea-things,
          and dragons, and bells,
The show rooms—*all* show,
          the sleeping rooms—cells.

But the *grand* Curiosity
          's not to be seen—
The owner himself—
          an old fat MANDARIN;
A patron of painters
          who copy designs,
That grocers and tea-dealers
          hang up for signs:
Hence teaboard-taste artists
          gain rewards and distinction,
Hence his title of ' TEAPOT'
          shall last to extinction.
I saw his great chair
          into which he falls—*soss*—
And sits, in his CHINA SHOP,
          like a large Joss;
His mannikins round him,
          in tea-tray array,
His pea-hens beside him,
          to make him seem gay.

It is said when he sleeps
   on his state Eider-down,
And thinks on his Wife,
   and about *half* a Crown;
That he wakes from these horrible dreams
   in a stew;
And that, stretching his arms out,
   he screams, Mrs. Q.!
He's cool'd on the M—ch——ss,
   but I'm your debtor
For further particulars—
   in a C letter.
You must know that he hates *his own* wife,
   to a failing;—
And it's thought, it's to shun her,
   he's now gone out
   SAILING.

A living teapot stands, one arm held out,
One bent; the handle this, and that the spout.

     Rape of the Lock.

    FINIS.

PUBLISHED BY WILLIAM HONE.

THE QUEEN'S LETTER TO THE KING. In octavo, Price 6*d.*
⁂ Orders should expressly state *Hone's* Edition.

THE DROPT CLAUSES OUT OF THE BILL AGAINST THE QUEEN. For Mr. Attorney General to peruse and settle. With a Refresher. By the Author of " THE QUEEN'S MATRIMONIAL LADDER." *Price Sixpence.*

THE QUEEN'S CASE STATED. By CHARLES PHILLIPS, Esq. Barrister at Law.
" You shall surely answer it, where the poorest rag upon the poorest beggar in this island shall have the splendour of your coronation garment."—*Vide Statement.* 8vo. 1s.

THE LAMENT OF THE EMERALD ISLE, on the DEATH of the PRINCESS CHARLOTTE. By CHARLES PHILLIPS, Esq.
☞ The remarkable Dedication of this beautiful Poem is to the Princess of Wales, as " the most desolate woman in the world ;" and foretels her Majesty's present situation in the loftiest strain of poesy and prophecy.—Seventh Edit. 8vo. 1s.

THE KING'S TREATMENT OF THE QUEEN shortly stated to the PEOPLE of ENGLAND.
" The press is the great public monitor—it shall extend to the farthest verge and limit of truth —it shall speak truth to the king in the hearing of the people."—*Curran's Speeches.* 8vo. 1s.

A TREAT FOR EVERY ONE ; or, The Political Dessert. A Satire.
" With wing untried, I've ventur'd thus to soar
" To subjects scarcely touch'd in Song before." 8vo. 2s. 6d.

THE POLITICAL HOUSE THAT JACK BUILT. With thirteen Cuts, viz.—The House that Jack built: the Wealth that lay in it ; the Vermin that plundered it ; the Thing to poison them ; the Public Informer ; the Reasons of lawless Power ; the Man all shaven and shorn ; the People all tatter'd and torn ; the guilty Trio ; the Word of Fear ; the Political Priest ; the Pen and the Sword ; the End—Liberty.——The Forty-fourth Edition, 8vo. 1s. *Fine Edition,* 2s. *Fine Coloured Edition,* 3s.

THE MAN IN THE MOON ; A Speech from the Throne to the Senate of Lunataria.—Also, A Political Christmas Carol, set to Music ; and " The Doctor," a Parody, written by the Right Hon. George Canning. With Fifteen Cuts, viz.:—The Man in the Moon—Going down—Carried down—The Grinder's Arms—Johnny Mooncalf—Steel Lozenges—Holy Alliance—Chaining the Press—Pulling the Trigger—Puffing—Put out the Light—Carol Music—Rats caught alive—The Doctor besquibbed—The Fraternal Embrace. The Eighteenth Edition 8vo. 1s. *Coloured Edition,* 2s.

THE OCEAN CAVERN : a Tale of the Tonga Isles. In Three Cantos.—The interesting story selected as the ground-work of this Poem, is in Mariner's Account of the Customs and Manners of the Inhabitants of the Tonga Islands. " The tale is beautifully related in the Poem, and occasions feelings " which a real bard only can raise. The author's name is not affixed. It has " been attributed to one who ranks highest amongst the children of Song."— *Handsomely printed in octavo, uniformly with Lord Byron's Poems,* 4s. 6d.

A NEW AND ENLARGED COLLECTION OF SPEECHES, by the Right Hon. JOHN PHILPOT CURRAN ; containing several of importance, in no former Collection, with MEMOIRS of Mr. Curran, and his PORTRAIT, *In one Volume Octavo,* 8s.
⁂ Eloquence has perhaps never suffered a deeper loss than by the imperfect manner in which the Speeches of this immortal Orator have been collected. The present edition embodies all his relics, and contains seven full speeches, with two extracts, in no other Collection. These grand efforts of oratorical genius leave the reader's mind in awful astonishment at the daring honesty of the intrepid advocate, and disclose scenes of incredible profligacy in the Irish Parliament, where the majestic figure of the Patriot rose in sublime and solitary pre-eminence. With Curran all is fire and energy. And these qualities, seconded by his honesty, fruitlessly exerted in his country's cause, make him exhibit in the midst of her expiring liberties, that most interesting of all human spectacles, " A Great Man struggling with the Storms of Fate." — If Genius, Integrity, Courage, and Perseverance could have redeemed Ireland from thraldom, Curran would have been known to posterity in the character of her saviour.

THE APOCRYPHAL NEW TESTAMENT, being all the Gospels, Epistles, and other Pieces extant, attributed in the first four Centuries, to JESUS CHRIST, his Apostles, and their Companions, and not included in the New Testament by its Compilers. Translated from the Original Tongues, and now first collected into One Volume.—8vo. 6s.

POLITICAL ESSAYS, WITH SKETCHES OF PUBLIC CHARACTERS, by WILLIAM HAZLITT, handsomely printed in one large Volume Octavo, 14s.

" Come, draw the curtain—shew the Picture."

This Series of energetic Essays is well described in the opening sentences of the preface: " I am no Politician, and still less can I be said to be a party-" man ; but I have a hatred of Tyranny, and a contempt for its Tools : and " this feeling I have expressed as often and as strongly as I could.—I have " no mind to have my person made a property of, nor my Understanding " made a Dupe of."—The Publisher conscientiously affirms, that there is more Original and just Thinking, luminously expressed in this Volume, than in any other Work of a living Author.

MURRAY'S SERMONS TO ASSES, TO DOCTORS IN DIVINITY, to LORDS SPIRITUAL, and to MINISTERS OF STATE, with the Author's Life and Portrait.—Civil and Religious intolerance were never more successfully exposed and ridiculed than by the close reasoning and sarcastic irony in these extremely able pieces. They are are now first collected into one large volume ; and form an Encyclopedia of Political truths, abounding with wit and humour, and the severest invectives of glowing patriotism.—8vo. 8s.

SIXTY CURIOUS AND AUTHENTIC NARRATIVES AND ANECDOTES respecting Extraordinary Characters ; Illustrative of the tendency of Credulity and Fanaticism ; exemplifying the Imperfections of Circumstantial Evidence ; and recording singular instances of voluntary Human Suffering, and Interesting Occurrences. By JOHN CECIL, Esq. In Foolscap-octavo. With an Historical Plate, 6s.

This is a most interesting little volume, either at home or abroad, and so entertaining and select, in its facts and language, as to render it a very agreeable companion, and an acceptable present.

THE PICTURE OF THE PALAIS ROYAL: describing its Spectacles, Gaming-houses, Coffee-houses, Restaurateurs, Tabagies, Reading-rooms, Milliners'-shops, Gamesters, Sharpers, Mouchards, Artistes, Epicures, Courtesans, Fillies, and other Remarkable Objects in that High Change of the Fashionable Dissipation and Vice of Paris. With Characteristic Sketches and Anecdotes of its Frequenters and Inhabitants. In a neat Pocket Volume with a large folding Coloured Engraving, 5s. Visitors to Paris should take it with them as a Guide and Mentor. Those who stay at home will be exceedingly amused by the singularity of manners it discloses.

Printed on Bank Post Paper, Price One Shilling.

AN ENGRAVED SPECIMEN OF A BANK NOTE—NOT TO BE IMITATED! with the BANK RESTRICTION BAROMETER, or Scale of Effects on Society, of the Bank-note System and Payments in Gold.—By the AUTHOR of " THE POLITICAL HOUSE THAT JACK BUILT."

₊ The EXAMINER says—" This Bank-note is by Mr. HONE, and ought to make the hearts of the Bank Directors (if they have hearts) ache at the sight.—It is altogether a curious Publication."

THE HISTORY OF PARODY.

The Materials for this Work are scattered over so extensive a range of Literature, that the difficulty of collecting them, in some measure baffled my hopes as to the time of Publication. My intentions, however, have always been to spare no pains in the Research ; and I confidently expect that the result will justify the labour I have expended upon it, and satisfy the strong curiosity I am conscious of having excited.—With a view to trespass as little as possible upon the patience of the subscribers, and at the same time to consult their convenience, I take this opportunity of announcing that the Work will appear in Monthly Parts, each containing at least five Engravings, and that it will probably be completed in Eight deliveries at 5s. each. I pledge myself that the first Part shall be published without fail on the 1st January next, and respectfully invite the names of Subscribers. The money to be paid on delivery of each Part.

Ludgate-Hill, 14th August, 1820.   WILLIAM HONE.

WILLIAM HONE'S CATALOGUE OF ANCIENT AND MODERN BOOKS, including many curious and scarce Articles, together with a large Collection of Old Tracts, particularly Trials, and also some engraved British PORTRAITS and PRINTS for Illustration, and a few PAINTINGS in Oil, now on Sale, at the Prices affixed to each Article, at No. 45, Ludgate Hill, London. —Catalogues Price 1s.

**THE QUEEN'S
MATRIMONIAL LADDER.**

PRINTED BY WILLIAM HONE,
LUDGATE HILL, LONDON.
Price (with the Pamphlet) One Shilling.

" NON MI RICORDO !"

&c. &c. &c.

" This will witness outwardly, as strongly as the conscience does within "

Cymbeline.

" Who are you ?"

Twenty=sixth Edition.

LONDON:

PRINTED BY AND FOR WILLIAM HONE, LUDGATE HILL

1820.

SIXPENCE.

☞ LOST, at the Court Martial, Signor **MY JOKEY'S MEMORY**, together with his Government Victualling Bill; both a little damaged, and of no use but to the owner. Whoever will bring them to the Publisher, in time to be restored to the Signor's disconsolate Mother, Mrs. *Leech*, shall be rewarded with a " *Non mi ricordo !*"

NOTE.

The Drawings for this Publication are
By MR. GEORGE CRUIKSHANK.

HONE'S NATIONAL TOY.

The most extensively embellished, and most rapidly selling production ever issued from the Press, Price 1s.

THE QUEEN'S MATRIMONIAL LADDER; a NATIONAL TOY. By the AUTHOR of the POLITICAL HOUSE THAT JACK BUILT. With 14 Step-Scenes; and Illustrations in Verse, with 18 other CUTS; viz. High and Low—He qualifies—declares—She accepts—He alters—imputes—She exculpates—emigrates—remigrates—consternates—He accuses—the Press watches—The British Lion awakes—He asks for his Crown and they give him the Bag—They degrade him—The End, Cats' Meat :—Teapot the Great—Gone Sailing.

Printed for WILLIAM HONE, Ludgate Hill; & sold by all the Booksellers in the United Kingdom.

" NON MI RICORDO!"

CROSS EXAMINED BY MR. BESOM.

WHO are you?   Non mi ricordo.

What countryman are you?—a foreigner or an englishman?   Non mi ricordo.

Do you *understand* ENGLISH?   No not at all.

Will the Oath you have taken *bind* you to speak the truth, or do you know of any other Oath *more* binding?

The TURNSTILE GENERAL objected to the question; upon which a discussion arose as to the nature of the Oath likely to bind the Witness, who appeared to be playing with a thread. The Witness was accordingly asked, by way of illustration, to what degree he thought the thread was *binding*, and whether he knew of any thing else *more* binding?

The Lord PRECEDENT FURTHERMORE said, if the Witness believed the thread he held was *binding*, that was sufficient.

The LORD PRECEDENT's opinion gave rise to a long discussion as to whether *more* binding was *binding*, and binding was *more* binding; which ended in a reference to the ERMINIANS, who delivered the following solemn opinion:—If the Witness shall answer that he thinks the bit of thread is *binding*, there is no doubt it *is* binding; but he cannot be asked if a cord is *more* binding, because he in fact, says that the thread itself is *binding*. If the Witness twists the thread round his little finger he is so far bound by it, and it is *binding*; and having done that, it is unnecessary to inquire whether a cord, round another part of his body, would be *more* binding.

Question over-ruled.

CROSS EXAMINATION RESUMED.

You are a master tailor, I think?   I was cut out for a tailor.

You have been a tailor, then?   I only follow tailoring as a mere amusement.

Fond of *Goose* I suppose—but pray Mr. Mere-amusement what is your business?   I was brought up a *Cabinet* maker.

What can you get at it?—are you a good hand? I can't say I am; I'm badly off; my *tools* are worn out.

What is your place of residence?

(Order Order).

The TURNSTILE GENERAL protested against the consequences of this mode of Examination.

Lord JURYMAN—Why does not the Interpreter give the Witness's Answer.

The Lord PRECEDENT FURTHERMORE—Because the Bench objects to the question.

Lord MUDDLEPOOL—Does the Turnstile General object to the question.

The TURNSTILE GENERAL. I do object to it, my Lord. This is perhaps the most important question that ever occurred. By this dealing out, the party is placed in such a situation as he never was placed in before.

Mr. BESOM—I ask him where he now lives, and the Turnstile General objects to this, because I do not put all the questions I might put, in a single breath.

The Lord PRECEDENT FURTHERMORE—I feel great difficulty—I doubt.

Lord WHEELBARROW thought there was a *great* deal in what the noble Lord had said; and *he* doubted.

CROSS EXAMINATION RESUMED.

How much money has been expended on you since you were born? Non mi ricordo.

What have you done for it in return? More less than more.

How do you get your living? I was waiter for some years at the Hotel *de Grand Bretagne,* and succeeded my father as head waiter at the *Crown* Inn.

What wages have you? Non mi ricordo.

Have you any perquisites? *Veils.*

Are you *head waiter,* or by what other name than head waiter you may be called, at the Crown Inn?

I am after building a new place called the *Wellington Arms,* and trying to be *Barrack-master*; if I dont gain the *Trial* I shall be glad to remain at the old *Crown.*

This answer appeared to excite considerable sensation,

The TWISTER GENERAL thought the meaning was, ' if I do n't gain what I attempt to gain.'

[The Short-hand writer was desired to read the answer, and the word *Trial* was retained as the correct translation.]

I do not ask what you are to be hereafter, but whether you are *still* head waiter at the Crown?

The head waiter is dismissed occasionally.

Are you married? More yes than no.

Do you live with your own wife? No.

Is she in this country? Yes.

Why did you marry? To pay my debts.

Then why did you part? Because my debts were paid.

Were you not up to the eyes in debt? Si Signor.

Are you not bound to manifest some gratitude towards those who have paid your debts?

The Interpreter said the witness was a mere *fanfaron*, and that he found it difficult, if not impossible, to explain to the witness's understanding what was meant by *gratitude*.

Cross Examination resumed.

Did not you write to your wife a licentious letter, called a letter of license?—*(Order, order.)*

I ask you again the cause of your separation? She left me.

On what account? I did not like her, and I told her I'd have nothing to do with *her* any more.

After that what did you do? Oh, I rambled about.

Where did you go? To Jersey and elsewhere.

Well, Sir, go on. Non mi ricordo.

Do you mean to say that you never went to Manchester Square? More yes than no.

Were you in the house on the footing of a private friend? No, not as a friend.

You mentioned your father just now :—you did not go in your father's *cart*, I presume ; in what sort of carriage did you go?   In the old yellow chariot.

How long did it take you to travel from Manchester Square to Richmond?   Non mi ricordo.

How many other places did you go to?   Non mi ricordo.

Is the Marquis of C. a married man?

(Order. Order.)

After you parted from your wife, on what terms did you live?   I've been *trying* to get rid of her.

Do you know what Matthew says (c. v. v. 32.)?

Matthew? Matthew? *(trying to recollect)*—what Matthew?—he's no friend of mine.

In what light do you consider your oath at the marriage ceremony?   A ceremony.

If your marriage oath has not bound you, can you expect people to believe you if ever you should take a solemn public oath?   More yes than no.

By the Roman law, a divorce was granted for Drunkenness, Adultery, and *False Keys :* what is your opinion of that law?

The TWISTER GENERAL said, that it was contrary to common sense to ask the witness's opinion about any *Law.*

How many Wives does *your* Church allow you? Non mi ricordo.

How many have you had since you separated from your own?   Non mi ricordo.

Are you a Member of the Society for the Suppression of Vice?   Yes *(with great energy).*

The Cross-examining Counsel said that the Interpreter had materially altered the sense of the last question; he had in fact asked, if the Witness was Member of the Society for the suppression of *Wives, (a loud laugh)* which Witness had eagerly answered in the affirmative.

The Witness's answer was expunged, and on the question being repeated correctly, he answered that he was told it was his duty to encourage the *Vice* Society, because it professed to diminish the influence of bad example.

Have they ever prosecuted you? Me!—*(with astonishment)*—they like *me* too well!

What do you mean then by *Suppression*—is your Society to prevent little vice from being committed, or great vice from being found out?

More Yes than No.

It was here moved by Lord LE CUISINIER, that 4 o'Clock, the hour of dinner, was arrived.

Another, in a maiden Speech, said, that during his long silence in that Court he had had leisure to observe, that 4 o'Clock in the *morning* was a more usual hour of adjournment.

Another considered that Lord LE CUISINIER's suggestion ought not to be entertained for a moment. We only exist in our formalities. If we suffer ourselves to be put a stop to by the motion, we may find that we are travelling round again into the obsolete usages of our early ancestors; which will be to describe a circle that must be generally considered as nothing less than a revolution! I therefore deprecate the least innovation, and move, as an amendment, that 4 o'Clock is *not* arrived.

The MASTER GENERAL of the *Black* Barracks at Exeter, rose without his wig, and declaring, upon the memory of his whiskers, that he had just heard it strike 4, he enquired whether the Clock was in *Order. (Loud and continued* cries of *hear hear.*)

The Home DOCTOR felt his pulse alarmingly quicken one and a fraction in the minute, and nervously said, that the clock was clearly guilty of a barefaced libel, and ought to be instantly held to bail for breach of the peace. The simultaneous action of all the Clocks throughout the nation and their open communication by circulars, was an index to the existence of an organized correspondence and a systematic affiliation. He trembled at the ' positive intelligence' he had received, that millions at that moment held their hands in an attitude ready to strike; but it was the proudest day of his life that he had so far succeeded by a *circular* movement of his own, as to enable his workmen to hold them to the peace for an hour together.

Lord BATHOS assured the Black-Barrack Master-General that the Clock *was* out of Order, and he congratulated the Home Doctor on his efficiency; but he thought they had not sunk low enough into the subject; for he had strong doubts whether the striking might not be construed into an overt act of High Treason, and if he saw any probability of being supported he should conclude with a substantive motion. Did not the Lord Precedent remember a Clock Case, in which, immediately after the chain had been locked up, a principal link suddenly disappeared? and whether, after the most minute inquiry, there was not every reason to believe from the best information that could be obtained at that

B

time, that that link had been *prigged? (Hear hear.)*
Take even the very last Clock Case, where the chain
was kept together with the greatest pains, and
the utmost care.   If the smallest link in that
chain had been *prigged,* it would have been fatal
to the works, and yet in that very case, two
days after the chain was locked up, a link was
obtained, which, if sooner discovered, would have
lengthened the chain to the necessary extent, and
brought home in the most conclusive manner the
guilt of the Clock.   He therefore moved that the
Clock be examined, and the chain kept in their own
custody, with liberty to add to the number of links.

Lord RATSTAIL with his usual animation seconded
the Motion.

Marquiz BOUDOIR moved as an Amendment, that
the Clock being in contempt, the *Black stick* be ordered to *walk him* in to-morrow.   Seconded.

Upon this Amendment the following Amendment
was moved and seconded, that the word ' to-morrow'
be expunged, and the word ' yesterday' be inserted
in its place.   *Ordered.*

CROSS EXAMINATION RESUMED.

Does the Witness recollect whether he was at
B———?   Non mi ricordo.

Who usually closed the Pavilion?   I did.

Was it so close as to exclude any person outside
from seeing what passed within, or was it partially
open?   It was quite closed—When I could not
close it with C******** entirely, I did it with other
pieces.

What do you mean by saying with other pieces?
I mean with other pieces of the same quality.

Symptoms of impatience were now expressed, with loud cries of *Withdraw, withdraw.*

Do you remember any thing particular occurring one night? No.

Do you not recollect whether a new wing was added during the time you and your mistress were absent? Non mi ricordo.

Do you know a certain Colonel Q.? Yes, he has *too* little mustachios.

Are you a sober man? More no than yes.

How many bottles a day do you drink. Non mi ricordo.

Do you drink six bottles? Non mi ricordo.

Five bottles? Non mi ricordo.

How many nights in the week do you go to bed sober? Non mi ricordo.

Are you sober now? More no than yes.

Where do you spend your mornings? At Curaçao.

Where do you spend your evenings? At the *Cat and Fiddle.*

What is your favorite dish? Trifle.

What is your favorite game? *Bag-at-L—*

What is your favorite amusement? The C.

After Dressing, Drinking, and Dreaming, what time remains for thinking? Non mi ricordo.

I hold in my hand a list of immense sums of money that have been advanced to you, how much have you left? None.

Well, but you have something to show for it? No.

How do you live? I have a *doll*-shop, and a large stable in the country, and some *cow*-houses in different parts.

Are not your favourite friends *horn*-boys and flash-men ?—*(Order, order.)*

Can you produce a certificate of good character from those who *know* you? Yes, from the *minister.*

Pho! pho! do n't trifle; can you from any *respect-able* person? More no than yes.

I understand you have the *scarlet* fever, do you not know that it ends here in a *putrid* fever? Non mi ricordo.

You have many companions and advisers, but have you to your knowledge one *real* friend in the world; and if not, why not? Non mi ricordo.

By what acts of your life do you expect you will be remembered hereafter? I shall not answer you any more questions; you put questions to me I never dreamt of.

Suppose every man in society were to do as you do, what would become of society; and what right have you to do so, more than any other man?—*(Wit-ness greatly agitated?)*

The Witness from the *Grillery* asked whether the *Cross* Examination was nearly concluded? *(Cries of* KEEP ON !)—Supposing that the business would close to day at 4 o'clock, he had made a private *assignation,* although he was quite ready to *stop* if necessary.

The Lord PRECEDENT FURTHERMORE was in favour of adhering to a square rule; he had not entered the Court till five seconds past ten by his *stop*-watch, in consequence of consulting with his Wife upon a motion-of-course which they had contemplated; and their further deliberation had been postponed until after the adjournment to-day. It was impossible to know what questions might turn out to be doubtful or doubtless; yet adjourning at Five o'Clock would gain a delay of six hours in the Week, and the *gaining of any thing* he considered very material in the present case.

An Adjournment then took place, the Witness remaining on

THE GRILLERY.

" The *Fat* in the Fire!"

CONSPIRACY.

WHEREAS a most abominable GANG, have caused to be published and promulgated throughout the Nation a description of the infirmities and necessities of our nature, of which decorum forbids the mention ; and also gross and inflaming allusions to the intercourse between the sexes, and wanton and shocking exposures relating thereto ; to the destruction of youthful innocence, to the shame and disgust of matron modesty, and to the horror of all heads of families : it is therefore proposed to call an immediate MEETING, for the purpose of considering the best mode of preventing an increase of this dreadful contamination, and of securing the ringleaders of the Conspiracy, and bringing them to condign punishment.

NEW VICTUALLING OFFICE.

TO CONTRACTORS.—Persons willing to supply this Establishment with CAST-IRON REPEATERS, having duplex Movements, according to the Working Models now in use as above, may send in Sealed Tenders, stating the number they can instantly supply for immediate use, and the price thereof at per hundred.

TO NACKERMEN.

THE old Hackney, Liverpool, who lately lost his paces, is glandered, gone blind, got cruel vicious, tried to kick his mistress's brains out, shattered himself to nothing, and is expected to go down with the staggers. Any body who thinks it worth while to send a *drag* to the Stable yard may have him for fetching.

TO MANGLERS—JUST LEAVING HIS PLACE.

A STOUT ABLE-BODIED IRISHMAN, for a long time a master hand at mangling ; when he begins there is no stopping him, and never tires. Can fold and smooth, and double and iron, all day. Will turn with any body. Was formerly a master in Dublin, where his mangling will never be forgotten. His Character may be had of any body there. Is very smooth spoken, of good address, looks like an upper Valet, and is a perfect devil at his Work. May be heard of at the Triangle in the Bird-cage Walk.

TO LAUNDRESSES, WANTS A PLACE.

AN old Woman accustomed to coarse things ; and work, however filthy, never comes amiss. Where she is now they find her in *ruin*, and she finds dishclouts ; but is leaving, being almost poisoned by printers' ink. To save trouble, will have nothing to do with cleaning the House. Is used to ironing, and putting by, in any quantities, and never tires at hanging up. Can have an undeniable Character from the Rev. Mr. Hay, and the Recorder of London.

STRAYED AND MISSING.

AN INFIRM ELDERLY GENTLEMAN in a Public Office, lately left his home, just after dreadfully ill-using his wife about half a Crown, and trying to beat her. He had long complained a great deal of his forehead, and lately had a leech put upon him. He was last seen walking swiftly towards the Horns without a Crown to his hat, accompanied by some evil disposed persons, who tied a great green bag to his tail full of crackers, which he mistook for sweetmeats, and burnt himself dreadfully. Every person he met in this deplorable condition tried to persuade him to go back, but in vain. He is very deaf and very obstinate, and cannot bear to be looked at or spoken to. It is supposed that he has been seduced and carried off by some artful female. He may be easily known by his manners. He fancies himself the politest man in Europe, because he knows how to bow, and to offer a pinch of snuff; and thinks himself the greatest man in Europe, because people have humoured him and let him have his own way. He is so fond of tailoring, that he lately began a suit that will take him his life to complete. He delights in playing at soldiers, supposes himself a cavalry officer, and makes speeches, that others write for him, in a field marshal's uniform. Sometimes he fancies himself ' Glorious Apollo,' plays ' Hailstones of Brunswick' on the base fiddle, and qualifies his friends to perform ' Cuckolds all on a row.' His concerns are very much deranged. Not long ago he imported a vast quantity of Italian images at enormous prices, upon credit, and hoarded them up in a waterside cotton warehouse. Since then, things have gone all against him, and he has been in a very desponding state. It is of the utmost consequence to himself that he should be at his post, or he may lose his place ; one of his predecessors some time ago having been cashiered for his misconduct. If this should meet his eye, it is earnestly requested that he will return to his duty, and he will be kindly received and no questions asked.

N. B. He has not a friend in the world except the advertiser and a few others, who never had an opportunity of speaking to him and letting him know the real state of his affairs.

1st September, 1820.

WHEREAS that well known old established Public House, (formerly a *free* house) called the POLITICAL HOUSE THAT JACK BUILT, has been feloniously entered into and damaged, and the property therein carried off to a large amount, by a numerous gang of desperate Villains, who, by various vile arts and contrivances, have not only kept possession thereof, but also of the Head Waiter, who was intrusted by Mr. BULL, the owner, with the management of the concern, and was a very promising young man when Mr. Bull first knew him, and might have done very well if he had followed the advice of his old friends, and not suffered these desperadoes to get him into their clutches; since when he seems to have forgotten himself, and by neglecting his duty sadly, and behaving ill to the customers who support the House, has almost ruined the Business, and has also dreadfully injured the Sign, which Mr. Bull had had fresh painted after he dismissed a former waiter for his bad manners. Whoever will assist Mr. Bull in bringing the offenders to Justice, will be doing a great service to the young man, and he will still be retained in his situation, unless he has actually destroyed or made away with the Sign, which Mr. Bull very much admires, it being a *heir-loom*. If offered to be pawned or sold it is requested the parties may be stopped, and notice given as above. As the young man has not been seen for some time, there is no doubt the ruffians have either done him a serious mischief, or secreted him somewhere to prevent Mr. Bull, who is really his friend, from speaking to him.

"What are you *at*? what are you *after*?"

THE END.

Printed by W. Hone, 45, Ludgate Hill.

The RADICAL. LADDER

THE

RADICAL LADDER;

OR,

HONE's

POLITICAL LADDER

AND HIS

NON MI RICORDO

EXPLAINED AND APPLIED,

THE DESIGNS OF THE RADICALS DEVELOPED, AND THEIR
PLANS TRACED,

A SATYRICAL POEM,

WITH COPIOUS NOTES.

———◆———

Printed at the Expense of the Loyal Association.

━━━━━

Printed by R. GRAY, Wine-office-court, Fleet-street.

PUBLISHED BY W. WRIGHT, FLEET STREET,

And to be obtained at all Booksellers.

━━━

1820.

Price One Shilling.

SELECTED FROM THE

LOYALIST AND ANTI-RADICAL.

THE

RADICAL AND INFIDEL CONTEST,

FROM THE SPA-FIELD RIOT

AND HONE'S TRIUMPHANT ACQUITTAL TO THE QUEEN'S
ELEVATION ON THE RADICAL LADDER;

IN WHICH

Hone's Pamphlets are explained and applied, the Designs of the Radicals
developed, and their Plans traced.

IN EIGHT BOOKS.

In the above Work will be introduced the Arrival of the Queen—an accurate Description of the Infidel Radical Chiefs—of the Spafield Riot —the Smithfield Assemblies—the Peterloo Engagement—Hunt's Triumphal Procession to the Metropolis—the Flight to the Moon—the Twopenny Subscription—the Canvass for Seats in Parliament—Hunt's Trial at York—the Catofield Defeat—the Royal Arrival—and the Queen's Elevation to the Summit of the Radical Ladder— adorned with appropriate Engravings and Caricatures, coloured.

RADICAL LADDER.

BOOK I.

The exiled Queen's Arrival—Conducted by the Quixotic Knight—Address to her Majesty—Radical Contest—The Political Ladder—Qualification—Declaration –Acceptation —Alteration—Imputation and Culpation—Emigration— Re-migration— Consternation-—Accusation—Publication—Me-diation—Rejection—Blindfolding and Leading—Demon-stration—Illustration—Indignation—Coronation— Degrada-tion—Radical Treason and Folly—Commiseration— Hunting —Expostulation—Mustering—Non mi ricordo.

ARRIVAL.

———————————" My past life
Hath been as continent, as chaste, as true,
As I am now unhappy.—Now behold me !
A fellow of the royal bed, with once
A moiety of the throne, a great King's daughter,
——————————— here standing,
To prate and talk of life and honour, 'fore
Who please to come and hear."   HERMIONE.

HARK ! whence is that shout which the populace raise ?
Lo ! a packet the *Queen* from long exile conveys,
She comes, and *kind Britons* a welcome resound,
And " Long live the Queen" shakes the welkin around !
A *chivalrous* homage calms Caroline's fears,
And her pathway to London *warm loyalty* cheers.

And who is the *Knight,* bold as Mancha's and
 meet,
Who *roams* land and sea *injured ladies* to greet ?
Whose *absolute wisdom* so skilfully knows,
Fit periods most suited, so wisely to choose ;—
When the Radical's noble, but fast *dying* cause,
Suppressed by such strict and such barbarous
 laws,
Their Leaders to Jail without mercy consigned,
And their Friends to dumb silence, so gagg'd
 and confined,
When the Radical Lugger by tempests hard tost,
O'erwhelm'd is fast sinking, and foundering and
 lost :—
Then conducts a Queen home the dull people to
 charm,
And all ranks in her cause with affection to
 warm.

ADDRESS TO HER MAJESTY.

On that *royal brow* may no cloud long remain,
May her *sun* in full radiance shine forth again :
I wish, like the *gold pure refined* from the fire,
This *fair one,* still fairer, the world may admire !✳
And hark ! as she moves mid the rapturous
 throng,
" Long, long, live the King !" is the theme of
 her song !†

 ✳ " Every virtuous mind wishes her innocent, and if innocent,
as a much injured woman to be pronounced so by the Peers of
England. It is every way best for the nation that she *should
be found so;* for innocence has not only the purity and power
of angels, but their harmlessness and benignity. The triumph
of an angel will be peaceable."   HORNE.
 † It is said, when the people shouted at Canterbury, " Long
live the Queen !" her Majesty put her head out of the carriage

Oh! why then should faction look out for its day,
And the long absent *Caroline* mark for its prey?
Oh! think not your *cause* she will madly espouse,
Nor her character lend your rebellion to rouse:
What! *Caroline* with *Cato-street Radicals* join?
No! she'll pause ere she pass the dread boundary
  line,
A party to marshal 'gainst *Albion's* King,
And the knell of her glory with madness to ring!
Shall *Caroline*, once great *Britannia's* joy,
Like *Helen* of Greece fire *another great Troy?*
Shall *civil discord* spread its furious flame,
Fann'd by *mock zeal* a *Queen's fair rights* to
  claim?
Shall *Britons* fam'd on *Waterloo's* dread plains,
Tarnish their fame e'en where the Monarch reigns?
Leave to the laws the Queen's *just rights* to prove,
Be yours to serve them both with duteous love.
A British Parliament its dauntless voice will
  raise,
Her fame to circle round with *Truth's* resplend-
ent blaze.

THE RADICAL CONTEST.

The war we thought closed—the cause lost and
  destroyed,
That Britons the radicals renounce and avoid,
That the cottager calm, sitting under his vine,
The laurel and olive would sweetly entwine,
That their Leaders imprison'd, the ruffians slain,
The Radicals never would rally again.

and shouted, " Long live the King!" Oh! had she continued
to act thus, instead of taking for her Counsel a *faction* who act
in hostility to her august Consort and Sovereign!

But the Radical Contest rekindled we view,
An *injured* Queen's rights to maintain and pursue!
What events may the nation so shaken betide!
What scenes of contention to contest allied:
I view in perspective a vista of spears,
The battle fast raging and Britain in tears!!*

THE POLITICAL LADDER.

My muse not so fast,—who taught you to climb
To a station so lofty, prophetic, sublime?
Who taught you to take such a vent'rous flight,
From the *earth* to the *moon* with each *radical
    wight?*
To guess their designs, and trace the *campaign*
From *Spafield* to *Smithfield* and *Waterloo* plain?
" I ne'er should have soar'd to a height so sublime,
Had not RHYMER produced me his LADDER to
    climb !
I well might before doubt my rash speculations,
And the Radicals well demand plain explanations;
But this new invented *Political Ladder*,
With gradations of infamy, sadder and sadder,
The designs of Reformists all legibly show,
Hunt or *Queen* to raise higher to bring a *King* low!
But the *treacherous* LADDER, like Haman's, may
    serve,
The authors to *raise* to a *height they deserve!*

* " My *only fear is*, that her Majesty is guilty, and will be
found so. The mischiefs, we fear, will arise from violent attempts to intimidate and oppose justice ; and what is this but a
loud proclamation of supposed crime? Or even after guilt is
proved, to make a furious outcry of injustice, and to push
things to every possible extremity."—HORNE.

THE LADDER ITSELF.

See a QUEEN on the Ladder, with dignified face,
Sitting jeering her Husband struck down in
  disgrace:
Then a history vile and malevolent tell,
A loyal brave nation to goad to rebel.

QUALIFICATION.

When the NATION ADVISING, a PRINCE takes a
  wife,
By kindred allied—the HOPE OF HIS´LIFE,
They shamefully shew him " o'ertoppled with
  debt, ·
" With wine and with women and duns on the
  fret."

DECLARATION.

As " *a prodigal son*" they with " perils surround
  him,
Vex'd, harass'd, bewilder'd," and try to confound
  him.

ACCEPTATION.

Then a CALUMNY raise, " that his debts *thrice* to
  pay,
" He from *Brunswick's walls* lures his *cousin*
  away."

ALTERATION.

Then causelessly quitting her unsullied charms,
Taking strangers, instead of his wife, to his arms!

IMPUTATION AND CULPATION.

Then *falsely* arraigning an *innocent* Wife,
" And *driving* her far from the home of her
    life :"—
Who knows not, that spite of all lies and eva-
    sions,
She quitted the realm, spite of urgent dissua-
    sions ! !

EMIGRATION.

Pursuing " the Wanderer," plotting, proscribing,
Her return then impeding, by threat'ning and
    bribing :
Who would not have thought, wishing no degra-
    dation,
She had better have *stay'd*, than *risk* losing her
    Station,
Than stand at the *bar*, tried for *crimes* of *such
    die*,
As the boldest must frighten and sink with a sigh :
Than to brave a whole nation in clearing her
    name,
And spread through the kingdom Rebellion's
    wild flame :
Far nobler and generous t' have *stayed* in *dis-
    grace*,
Than to *flood* a whole Empire to *wash clean* her
    face.

REMIGRATION.

Now steers *German* HELEN to Britain's great
    Troy,
Rowed swift through the waves by her *Alderman
    Boy*,

The *Royal Whale* vainly his water-spouts pouring,
And sword-fish, and sharks, and the ocean-wave
roaring.

CONTSERNATION.

She comes ! with her *torch-light* to kindle a *fire*,✱
Which the kingdom envelopes with *clouds* dark
and dire !

✱ " Urged on by unprincipled and merciless instigators, her
Majesty, to use the insinuation of the old *Times*, has *invaded*
the land : and, to judge by the attitude assumed by herself and
her partisans, is prepared to wrestle with her Sovereign for his
sceptre and diadem, which he cannot lose without loss of life."
                                                            HORNE.
   " Who was there that did not once most strongly feel for the
Queen as the forsaken wife of youth ?   And a generous people
mingled their regrets with her tears.   But when our ears became more wounded with the tale of her *levities*, than our hearts
had been with her *woes*, and a public investigation of imputed
criminalities was the result, we sighed as well as rejoiced, when
her very acquittal was mingled with censure.   When she threw
herself into the arms of opposition the tide of opinion began to
turn against her.
   " That she could not conciliate the affections of her husband
was her *misfortune;* but when she braved the resentment, and
disturbed the Government of her Prince, it was her *fault*.   While
we felt for her as *Men*, we disapproved her conduct, as *loyal subjects*.   Still, while she continued in England, the Princess kept
a strong hold on the feelings of wise and good men.   But when
Englishmen, returning from travel, and Foreigners, touching on
our coast, loudly circulated the tale of national dishonour, what
could the Regent do but inquire, by an honourable commission,
into the truth of an infamy so publicly talked of?   The results
of those inquiries are partly before the public; and the keeping
them back so long, and the reluctance with which they were
produced, argue delicacy, feeling, consideration, and honour."
                                                            HORNE.

B

DESERTION.

But where is *Bergami*, and all her *tried* friends,
Who graced all her flight to the earth's utmost
ends?
Who, in Europe, and Asia, and Afric's broad plains,
Still faithful adher'd, *reaping harvests* of gains?
Such adherents must *foes* to her cause have con-
verted,—
They remain'd, when *base Britons* their Queen
had deserted!
Ye Friends of the Queen! you *sadly* defend her,
Not to bring to her trial *such friends* to befriend
her!
Bergami her *purity* loud would proclaim,
And clear from aspersion her *untarnished* fame!
He would manfully lift up his *whip* or his sword
To defend the *pure* name of his Caroline ador'd!

ACCUSATION.

She who smiles at base slander with dignified face
Should have brought such *tried friends* her ac-
cusers to face!
The *mob* she allures, and *quizzes* her King,
And her *ridicule* shakes at the charge he may
bring.
Now a *watchman*, he finds her out false to his bed,
· And *precedents* seeks *not* to cut off her head.＊

* Who can charge the Sovereign with aiming a blow at his
Consort's life? Nay, we know he was anxious in the former investigation, and has shown himself not less so in this inquiry, not
to pursue her conduct as a capital offence.

PUBLICATION.

Guy Fauxes-like, *not* trying to blow up his wife,
Though a Traitor-like Leader of Radical strife!

MEDIATION.

See the whole British Parliament courteously stand,
To *quench* the red *Torch* at her gracious com
    mand!†
See the *foe* of oppression, poor *Africa's friend*,
Lab'ring *England* and *Caroline's* fame to defend!
Then—then, was the time to disperse the *black
    cloud*,
And, with " snowy-white" vesture, her frailties
    to shroud!
Then, then was the moment the patriot to shew,
And, for *national good*, a *mere form* to forego!
Then, then was the time to cry " Long live the
    King!"
And with " Long live the Queen!" for the welkin
    to ring.
Oh! *then* might contentions, fast waning, have
    ceas'd,
And the nation from tumult and care been
    releas'd.

REJECTION.

But will Radicals suffer this high-burning flame,
Rekindled and blazing by Caroline's name,
Just catching the throne, and *John Bull's* an-
    cient house,
T'expire, like the mountain producing a mouse!

---

† Who that reflects on all that has been done to avoid the investigation, but must allow that King, Lords, and Commons,
have deprecated it to the utmost, and would have put up with
any thing, on tolerable terms, rather than provoke the perils of it.

No ! Caroline, rais'd to the Ladder's high top,
Supported shall stand to lift the mob up.
Lo! thus she replies ; " Your affection I feel,
And your uncorrupt care for the general weal ;
But ne'er will I smother this national fire,
Which the throne, fast consuming, may raise me
     still higher!
No, no ! I have pass'd o'er the *Rubicon* stream !
And onward I'll go, should the sword round me
     gleam !

BLINDFOLDING AND LEADING.

See! the Radicals, blinding the *poor beguiled*
     Queen,
Lead her onwards, o'er path-ways enamell'd and
     green,
To a *pile* lofty rais'd, like the *widow'd* Gentoo's,
To ascend, and to *sink down* in similar woes !
Like Dido, enrag'd at Æneas, who left her,
Whose madness of life and of kingdom bereft her,
Poor Caroline, I fear, a destructive pile climbs,
Help'd by Radicals up, who may perfect their
     crimes
In putting the torch to the fuel prepar'd,
And consuming the throne which the Queen
     would have shar'd.

DEMONSTRATION.

Behold the vile proof! see the pride of our isle,—
Fam'd Wellington, whose wonderful courage and
     skill
The tide of war turn'd from the overwhelm'd na-
     tions,
And Britain deliver'd from dire devastations.

Who on Waterloo's plains stood firm as a tower,
While numberless legions the bloody field scour,
With prowess unyielding resisted their might,
And snatched with bold hand a triumph for right;
Who, crown'd with the laurels of dearly-bought
        fame,
As her patriot hero to Albion came :—
See the Gen'ral, who Europe's fell foes all defeated,
By Radicals insulted, malign'd, and ill-treated !*
But from true British bosoms shall never be
        driven
Great Wellington, the Guardian sent us by
        Heaven.
Behold the vile proof, too, in Jervis the good,
Who the friend of the poor and of righteousness
        stood,
His house is attacked by the Cheltenham mob:
How, Denham, could you coolly look on the job!
The church is assail'd, broken open, profan'd,
And the bells madly rung by the radical band !
See Cunningham, the eloquent Pleader for Truth,
The exemplary Pastor, distinguish'd by worth,
Wisely warning his flock 'gainst the treacherous
        foe,
Who, pretending their weal, would involve them
        in woe,

* What further proof of the spirit and designs of the Radicals
is wanted than their insolence towards the Duke of Wellington,
in his return from the House of Lords.   Every reflecting
mind must be convinced that the Duke of Wellington and Mr.
Wilberforce were actuated by no other motive in the confer-
ences which they held with her Majesty's counsel, and in the
address of the House of Commons, on the business pending in
Parliament, than a sincere desire to terminate the proceedings
against her Majesty in the manner most advantageously for
herself and the nation at large.   Their insolence towards both
these characters proceeded, therefore, from gross misunder-
standing and delusion, or from radically bad principles.

Then the cowardly Radicals, by truth overcome,
Would, like savages, steal with a dirk on his
    home.*
Heav'n extend o'er its friends an impregnable
    shield,
And with peace and with gladness their length-
    ened days gild.

INDIGNATION.

My Muse now their purposes faithfully trace,
And shew the whole system, black, bloody and
    base!
The old British Lion with fury they'd wake,
Not to *burst bags of smoke*, but the *King* to
    unmake!

CORONATION.

The King they would jeer, and " belie all his
    history,
As a mis-rule of force, folly, taxing, and mystery."
His wishes they'd brand as " with law incom-
    patible,"
And treasonously say " his Crown's uncomatable."
This ditty they bandy to each saucy wag—
" He ask'd for a Crown and they gave him a
    Bag!"

---

* Who knows not how these seeming friends of innocence, liberty, and order, attacked, with brutal and unmanly violence, the truly pious, patriotic, and Rev. Mr. Jervis, of Chelten-ham, because, forsooth, he did not choose to set the bells a-ringing when Denham happened to arrive there! We hope the report is not true that Britons have disgraced themselves by threatening the Rev. Mr. Cunningham!

DEGRADATION.

What more degradation will Rhymer attempt?
What farther abuse? from *treason* exempt!
He sets him hung round with a sheet on a stool,
For the finger of scorn to deride as a fool!
But too lenient and kind this high degradation—
The *Ladder* breaks under the Head of the
       nation!
Till, fell'd and destroy'd by the radical crew,
He is drawn in a barrow, the cats crying " mew!!"

RADICAL TREASON AND FOLLY.

Shame, Britons! Awake! Shall your Monarch
       be hurl'd,
By raddical scribblers, as *scum*, through the
       world!
Shall a Sovereign, who treads in the steps of his
       Sire,
Be dethron'd by the hands of base radical ire!
Shall Britons be seen to low Radicals bending,
And unite for the Queen, 'gainst the Monarch
       contending!*

* " The bravest, wisest, and best, must lament to see a Queen of England at the head of such a mixed, furious, and unprincipled faction. Let what will happen, the Country will do her duty to the last. Old Horace, though a heathen, spoke nobly :—' Dulce et decorum est pro patriâ mori;' and of one thing we may be certain, should any die in the contest, they will be far more happy than they who should survive to crouch beneath the tyranny of a triumphant faction. All see the *possibility* of an appeal to the sword. The Radicals contemplate its probability, and confidently anticipate its success. —It proves weakness, and *conscious* weakness, to spread unnecessary alarm ; but when great danger exists, while wisdom dissembles whatever can increase that danger, the higher and middle classes should be made to feel the *necessity* of union, courage, and exertion."—*Horne.*

COMMISERATION.

What's the Queen to Reformists ?—As Queen
    was to France.
Round her head and her Consort's they'd equally
    dance.
They care not for Caroline, for King, nor for
    Queen,
A *pretext* they want their intentions to screen.
" The QUEEN !" is the Radicals' rallying cry,
A Queen bears the standard the King to defy !

HUNTING.

A Royal Stag hunted by blood-hounds is seen ;
But not chaste Diana, the bold huntress Queen.
They would hunt him, till thirsty and panting
    for breath,
And then slake his thirst with the chalice of
    death !*
The system pursued is the KING TO DETHRONE,
A system which thousands, too late, may bemoan.
A HUNT or a THISTLEWOOD, COBBETT or QUEEN,
Is all one to the *Radical Ruffians*, I ween,
My Muse the whole system shall faithfully trace,
And develope its spirit to shame and disgrace.
May Britons attend, and the warning receive,
Ere ruin remediless their hopes undeceive !

EXPOSTULATION.

Shall madness yon Castle with outrage assail ?
Where justice has reigned, shall disorder prevail?

---

* " A deadly chalice, mingled by human malice with every
poisonous ingredient, is now forced on the lips of England's
King."—*Horne.*

Shall that Castle, whence truth and fair equity
    flow'd,
And wise counsels extended our glory abroad,
Be shattered by anarchy's ravaging arm—
Be the fort whence the despot may scatter alarm?
Shall a King be dethron'd, and his council
    destroyed,
And the Kingdom with Radical Meetings
    annoy'd?
Shall a City, for commerce and wealth so
    renown'd,
With palaces, temples, and glory so crown'd,
With smoke be envelop'd by radical zeal,
And to ashes reduc'd for the general weal!
Its RELIGION abolish'd, its MINISTERS *slain*,
That *virtue* may *smile* o'er the land *once again!*
To raise up the Queen, shall the Monarch be
    be hurl'd
From the Throne of his Fathers, and driv'n
    through the world?
Shall Radicals reign and revel o'er right?
Shall justice be spurn'd, low bending to might?
Shall the voice of the Judges, the Commons, and
    Lords,
Be silenc'd by barbarous radical swords?
Forbid it, kind Heav'n! let Britain review
The radical war, and more wisdom pursue,
Let Law and Religion victorious reign,
And the fell demon Discord for ever be slain!

EXPLANATION.

Twelve months since the HUNTS*man* conducted
    his rabble,—
Now a poor deceiv'd *Queen* leads the radical
    squabble;

c

'Tis the throne they detest, 'tis this they would fire,
And the *King* and the *Queen* in the flames must
   expire!

MUSTERING.

My Muse now the *rise* of this *contest* reveal,
And the *Captains'* great names with their *History*
   tell;
Behold the notorious, wise, and grand leaders
Of the radical cause, the redoubtable pleaders!
The *Bookselling Rhymer*, the *Deist Carlile*,
The *Huntsman* who marshall'd the troops, rank
   and file;
The *Doctor* with *potions* t' inebriate the mob,
The *Thistle* to *goad* them to murder and rob;
The *Press*, with a weight t' impress the deep seal
Of *Rebellion*, which *Harrison* preach'd with such
   zeal;
The *Dwarf* from his corner his arrows fast shooting,
And *Sir Frank* and *Sir Charles* truth and order
   uprooting;
The *Porcupine* with scribblings and *Paine's* de-
   cayed bones,
The people to please with his jokes or his groans;
The chivalrous Knight, with adventures surprising,
As those t' Hudibras or Don Quixote arising!*

---

* " We must be content to be stigmatized emphatically by
all as the *mad nation;* a people who contemptibly tilt with
peaceable windmills, which grind the bread of life, mistaking
them for the giants of tyranny and oppression. Never did the
wit and satire of Cervantes imagine any thing more ludicrous
than what we are acting in real life. The Quixotism he exposes
is comparatively innocent and merely ludicrous. Our's is pure
crime and sport for devils. Don Quixote and honest Sancho
Panza, have been, and shall be, a *healthful laugh* to Europe;

INVESTIGATION and NON MI RICORDO.

Who rebellion at *Spafield* and *Peterloo* plann'd?
Who the *Radical Lugger* so valiantly mann'd?
Who *sapiently* laugh'd at *green bags full of smoke?*
Who gloried in making his *Sovereign a joke?*
Who mechanics inveigled at *soldiers* to *play*,
To plot against Britain in ruinous fray?
O! " non mi ricordo" the Radicals cry,
And with " non mi ricordo" their system deny!

Who, when the *train'd ruffians* were *timely* re-
     strain'd,
A fierce undistinguishing *massacre* feign'd?
Who, when law and religion imprison'd its *foes*,
As enslav'd by fell tyrants so fiercely uprose?
Who, mourn'd that the *madmen*, wide *scattering*
     fire,
Were *safely secur'd* in imprisonment dire?
Who, when the *assassins* were taken and slain,
Said the *Cato-street innocents* were murder'd for
     gain?
Who, when the fell cause was just sunk in the
     mire,
And the Radical Demon was like to expire,
By Albion's Lion fierce struck to the ground,
To restore and revive him *lost C—r—ne* found?
O " non my ricordo" the Radicals cry,
And with " non mi ricordo" their system deny!

but what eulogy shall we pass on Earl Grey and Alderman
Wood?"—HORNE.

    The impartiality and manly sense of justice which Earl Grey
displayed in the House of Lords, on the 17th August, must
exempt him from the full force of the above sarcasm. The
Earl declared, that no motives either of favour, fear, or reward,
should deter him from an investigation of the truth, and a sub-
mission to the dictates of justice in this important inquiry.
" O sic omnes!"

Who, when land was all gone and money all
spent,
With *Gerard*-like wisdom his eloquence lent;
Which, with usury rich, might his labours repay,
And, with Royalty's smile, gild his dark cloudy
day?
Who, when *mines* fail'd to bring him the wealth
of Peru,
And threaten'd a ruin which his house would
undo,
With *absolute wisdom* to Royalty fled,
Whose Midas-like touch might give gold for his
lead,
And, with places and pensions, his fortune's re-
store,
And bring him the cheers of the mob, as before?
O " non mi ricordo" the Radicals cry,
And with " non mi ricordo," the fact would deny!

Who, to hail revolution, a *dinner* prepare,
And invite all the kingdom *its blessings* to *share?*
Who th' example so manfully dared to propose,—
At the National Anthem to turn up the nose?
Who, " God save the King," by Britons long
hail'd,
With hisses receiv'd, and with curses assail'd?
Who, the *goblet o'erflowing*, significant crown'd,
And, with *Judas-like* " hail," struck the *crown* to
the ground?
O " non mi ricordo" the Radicals cry,
And with " non mi ricordo," the system deny!

Who, that *Courier* and Queen never slept near
each other
Averr'd,—but were pure, just as sister and brother?
Who, *Times*-like, derided such filthy inventions,
As Italian conspiracies, falsehoods, conventions?

And who, the next day, *Hownam*-like, so con-
    fess'd,
That, for five weeks, *together* they retired to their
    rest ?
Who said, the same tent o'er Bergami extended,
Which so *safely* the pure *Queen of England de-*
    fended?
O " non mi ricordo," the Radicals cry,
And with " non mi ricordo," their system deny !

    Who *valiantly* boasted the business he'd *smash*,
And down all the hopes of the government dash ?
Who, with *sailor-like* fortitude, fearlessly brav'd
The whole battery of truth, and for Caroline crav'd
Acquittal, from all the base charges preferr'd
By lying Italians, with filthiness smear'd?
Who, *Flynn*-like, confounded to see his own lies,
Quite powerless and trembling, shrunk from the
    eyes
Of piercing observers, who mark'd his false tongue,
As he fell, at the knell of his infamy rung ?
O " non mi ricordo" the Radicals cry,
And with " non mi ricordo" the truth they deny !

    Who confess'd that reports were so shocking
        and sad,
That to stay with the Queen she opin'd was too
        bad,
Lest her character *pure* should incur a deep *stain*,
Which she long might be toiling to wash out again ;
Yet, with *lady-like honour*, most firmly declar'd it,
That the Queen, undeserving such infamy,—shar'd
    it?
Who dar'd to the proof all the witnessing band ?
Who resolv'd, spite of calumny, boldly to stand ?
Who, in person, determin'd the charges to meet ?
Who rode to the house, all the populace to greet ?

And who, when a *too knowing witness* appear'd,
By *intimate services* greatly endear'd,
Convulsively scream'd out, " What, Theodore,
    Thou !"
And frantic *flew off*, like a shaft from a bow ?
And " non mi ricordo" the Radicals cry,
And, with " non mi ricordo," detection defy !

But conscience, whose voice ev'n the dullest
    must hear,
Says, who flee but the *guilty*, with cowardly
    fear ?
What Englishman *faints* in a *cause* that is *good ?*
'Tis the *perjured*, who *faulter* where *truth* would
    have *stood*.
Who, *underplots* frames, with such *Pearson*-like
    skill,
And, with *Absolute wisdom*, the mob to beguile,
To *stir up addresses* to a chaste injured Queen,
And with *loyalty's mantle* the dagger to screen ?
Who the *soldier's* proposed to *seduce* from their
    duty,
By promise of pensions, of lands, and of beauty ?
Who the *price* of rebellion at *twelve acres* fix'd,
When at Birmingham he with his kin-traitors
    mix'd ?
O " non mi ricordo" the Radicals cry,
And with " non mi ricordo" their system deny !

Who with treasonous shouts makes the welkin
    to ring,
And then a *queer zeal* shews for Albion's King ?
Who *hatches a plot* 'gainst th' omnipotent people,
To urge them to pull down the throne and the
    steeple ?
O " non mi ricordo" the Radicals cry,
And with " non mi ricordo" their system deny.

Could ought but *Pearsonic* sagacity see,
And *Gerard*—or *Wood*-headed *wisdom* agree,
That a Loyalist 'ere would the Government serve,
By tempting the people from duty to swerve?
Who with merriment foul makes the festive board
      ring,
While his tales 'gainst the Queen point their sharp
      deadly sting?
And who with a phiz, as a *Doctor's*, demure,
Swears the Queen was all virtue and grace—he is
      sure?
O " non mi ricordo" the Radicals cry,
And with " non mi ricordo" would cover the lye!

Who rode on an ass round the lawns and the
      ground,
And his *man*, at the grotto, with C---r--l--ne found?
Who, before his compeers, a peer's high honour
      pledg'd?
That no harm in the Princess could e'er be al-
      ledg'd?
O " non mi ricordo" the Radicals cry,
And with " non mi ricordo," their conscience
      belie!

Who said 'twas unmanly to pry into sin,
And to blazen and test it, like *Hownam* and *Flynn*?
Who, with *Calcraft urbanity*, wisely declar'd,
That from law, and its forms, should a *woman* be
      spar'd?
What *liberty-lovers* in London's fair town,
Who, in cellars and garrets, thick lodge up and
      down,
Would not lay out three shillings and eightpence
      a-piece
To purchase shoes, feathers, and shining pelisse;

And *loyally* travel in coaches and four,
To establish a code never thought of before ;
The brave Queen to applaud, whom none should
    disparage,
Whoever she favours, whatever her carriage?
Who is there that will, for a moment, refuse,
An example to choose, which *their slips* will ex-
    cuse?
From *Lad*-lane, *Grub*-street, Philpot-lane, *Hug-
    gin*-Green,
To *Bartholomew*-close, crowds will visit the Queen!
Her acquittal, with vociferations, demand,
And trumpet her praises through every land ! !
And *who* on the Continent sounds it amain?
Who at Lucca, and Florence, and famous Milan,
Gaily glitters with livery of scarlet and gold,
In his chariot, with valets and *couriers*, bold?
Who, *en Prince*, travels fast to Bologna chateau,
The estate Royal Caroline gave to her *beau?*
O " non mi ricordo," still, still will you cry?
'Tis the *ci-devant* footman, who pleased a Queen's
    eye?

Who sat at the table with Britain's fair Queen,
And reclin'd on her sofa beneath the tent-screen?
Who sustained her by land and by sea on his arm—
Who reaps his reward on his *gaily*-earn'd farm?*

* See Letter in *Courier*, for 19th Oct., dated Hackney, containing a quotation from the Letter of a confidential friend,
dated 24th ultimo, conveying the happy tidings of Bartolomeo
Bergami's present prosperity :
    " We left the baths of Lucca, Florence, and, after staying a
few days to have the carriage repaired, arrived on our route to Bologna.   Bergami, the Baron of such reputed fame, break-
fasted at the same hotel at which we were staying. He was
going from Milan to the estate purchased for him (as it is said)
by his Royal *Mistress*. He travelled " *en Prince*." Two cou-

O " non mi ricordo!" the Radicals cry,
And with " non mi ricordo" each tale they deny

Oh! why then did Hownam and Flynn so con-
spire
With Majocchi and Dumont to smear her with
mire !

riers preceded him, another servant sat on the box of the carriage,
and a valet rode inside with him. His *livery* was *scarlet* and
gold. An express from England just overtook him."

Only think, ye friends of the Queen, —a late courier, now
Baron Bergami! O tempora! O mores! What are his *ostensible*
services, that he should have been so rewarded ? Before the
Queen be received into the affections of Englishmen, and share
the honours of her high station, it is not too much to ask for an
explanation of this mysterious elevation—a *ci-devant footman* to
be enriched till he can adopt the livery of the Royal Family of
England! How many poor families might be relieved and supported with the wealth which the country subscribed to heap on
such a low favourite ! How much better might these thousands
per annum have been laid out in promoting the Charities, which
our *abused Government* patronizes:---such as relieving the silk-
weavers of Spitalfields---the poor houseless wanderer---the
wretched, perishing sailor---the decayed artizan and manufac-
turer---the reduced tradesman---the afflicted peasant !

THE
ANTI-INFIDEL ; or, MONTHLY REFLECTOR :
In refutation of the prevailing Errors of the Day ; with a
RETROSPECT ; published the first Day of the Month,
with Plates, priee 1s. 6d. by W. Wright, Fleet-street, at the
Expense of the Loyal Association.

R. GRAY, Printer, 7, Wine Office Court, Fleet Street.

235

Just Published, Nos. 1, 2, 3, 4, *and* 5, *of*

THE

LOYALIST;

OR,

ANTI-RADICAL;

CONSISTING OF

THREE DEPARTMENTS:

SATYRICAL, MISCELLANEOUS,

AND

HISTORICAL.

1. SATYRICAL.

The History of the Radical Contest, from the Spafields' Riot and Hone's Acquittal to the Queen's Elevation on the Radical Ladder, a Mock-Heroic Poem, illustrated with Copious Notes, and ample Descriptions of the Principal Leaders.

2. MISCELLANEOUS.

Communications, Notices, Poetic Effusions, Anti-Radical and Anti-Infidel Selections and Reviews.

3. HISTORICAL.

Sketches of Queen Caroline, by a Tourist on the Continent.—Illustrations of genuine Royal Virtue, in Visits to Claremont, Kensington, Windsor.—Weekly Retrospect, &c.

WITH ENGRAVINGS AND CARICATURES, COLOURED,

BY THE FIRST ARTISTS.

Printed at the Expense of the Loyal Association.

TO BE PUBLISHED EVERY SATURDAY, PRICE SEVENPENCE-HALFPENNY, OR
TWO SHILLINGS AND SIXPENCE EACH MONTHLY PART.

" England hath long been mad and scared herself:
The brother blindly sheds the brother's blood.—
Abate the edge of traitors, gracious Lord!
That would reduce these bloody days again,
And make poor England weep in streams of blood!
May civil wounds be stopp'd, peace live again!
That she may long live here—God say, Amen!"

SHAKESPEARE.

LONDON:

Printed by R. GRAY, Wine-office-court, Fleet-street.

PUBLISHED BY WILLIAM WRIGHT, FLEET STREET,

AND SOLD BY CHAPPELL, PALL-MALL; ROWE, AMEN-CORNER;
AND ALL OTHER BOOKSELLERS.

NEW PILGRIM'S PROGRESS;

OR,

A JOURNEY TO JERUSALEM.

𝔖econd 𝔈dition.

LONDON:

PRINTED FOR W. WRIGHT, 46, FLEET-STREET.

1820.

[*Price One Shilling.*]

PREFACE.

LEST the reader should be scandalized by the ideas which the following cuts may suggest, the Author thinks it necessary to say, that he has in this work, with the most scrupulous nicety, purified the details which have been from day to day for three weeks legally and necessarily brought before the public eye.

THE EMBARKATION.

"The scarfed barks put from her native bay,
"Hugged and embraced by the strumpet wind."
SHAKSPEARE.

DISGUSTED with this formal nation,
    Which at light amusement cavils,
A high-born lady quits her station,
    And sets out upon her travels.

THE EMBARKATION.

At present by a gouty knight led,
  Seeking abler aid, she jigs
In all the youthful bloom of white lead,
  Patent rouge, and auburn wigs.

Whitbread in vain, (her ancient crony,)
  Puts his most forbidding face on,
She spurns his counsel, chinks her money,
  And embarks on board the Jason.

All the incidents I mention,
  Remind one of a tale of Greece,
The ship, the wig, the monstrous pension !
  'Tis Jason and the GOLDEN FLEECE.

HIRING.

"I am a drudge to toil in your delight."

SHAKSPEARE.

THE Lady condescends to see
    The courier; and to question too;
"What is your sir-name?"—Bergami!
    "Your Christian name?"—Bartholomew.

HIRING.

" Come, honest Bergami, let *me* know

   " Where you've in service been already ?"

" Madam, I've lived with Mrs. Pino,

   " And I rode and drove my lady !"

The knowing eyes of the beholder

   Distinguish thro' his tatter'd dress,

A strength of limb, and breadth of shoulder,

   Suited to an Hercules.

" What for Mrs. Pino you did,

   " You for me shall also do—

" Wages, boarding,—all's concluded !

   " You shall RIDE and drive ME too."

RIDING POST.

' Oh, wicked speed, to post

" With such dexterity to luxurious sheets."

SHAKSPEARE.

DRIVE on, drive on, I pray you do ;

Of speed now make your best ;

For I am faint and fev'rish too,

And needs would take my rest.

RIDING POST.

Drive on and reach the nearest place,
　Where English do not stay ;
For I will shun that hated race,
　And drive some other way.

Drive on, the suite are just in view ;
　Drive fast, as fast may be
For I must e'en get but to you,
　Or you get in to me.

Then Berghy whipped with might and main,
　And reached the welcome door,
And with his back tow'rds her—again,
　He never drove her more.

C

A RURAL WALK.

"More than to wait upon your royal walks,
"Your bed—your board."

SHAKSPEARE.

NEVER sure on earth was seen a
    Pair, so formed the eye to charm,
Whiskerandos, Tilburina,
    Queen and Lacquey, arm in arm.

A RURAL WALK.

She to gather blooming posies,
   Through her private garden roves,
Yet beyond the sweetest roses,
   Tu-lips of Bergami she loves.

Lady Charlotte looks astounded,
   With her can she longer dwell?
Couriers, Campbells, thus confounded,
   " Chaqu'un a son *goût*," cries Gell.

Now the suite begin to doubt her,
   She looks out for fresh recruits,
Nothing *English* left about her
   But a book *of cheques on* COUTTS.

DELICATE ATTENTIONS.

"How sweetly do you minister to love."

SHAKSPEARE.

Now no more a liveried rider,
　　See promoted Bergami,
In her chaise he sits beside her,
　　Hand to hand and knee to knee.

DELICATE ATTENTIONS.

Not the hands and knees alone
　　They mingle ; if we credit Sacchi,
The fingers of the fair have known
　　All the proportions of the lacquey.

Not for a moment will she free him
　　From her touch or from her sight :
Happy all day long to see him,
　　And to feel him all the night.

Nay, upon a queer occasion,
　　When affection waxed colder,
She, in dread of an evasion,
　　Deigns to be his *bottle-holder !*

THE MASQUERADE.

" And with presented nakedness,

" Outface the wind.———————"

SHAKSPEARE.

FLAUNTING at a Masquerade

   See the chaste Historic Muse.

Attired by Berghy's blushing aid

   In not a stitch—except her shoes.

THE MASQUERADE.

This strange costume may seem a myst'ry;

But *this* is her excuse I take it:

Truth is the real Muse of Hist'ry,

And Truth we know is mother-naked.

All the Italians at the ball

Wonder what such a sight can mean:

If it be History at all

It must be that of Messaline.

The English lost in wonderment

To see a Muse so bare and plump,

Fancy she means to represent

Cobbett's new Hist'ry of the *Rump!*

NEW ACQUAINTANCE.

" Poor furniture and mean array."

SHAKSPEARE.

EXALTED by this magic stroke

    The Baron feels a bold impatience

To send away the English folk

    And introduce his own relations.

NEW ACQUAINTANCE.

" There, madam, is my little br.ther

" And that's my sister out of place,

" And there you see my honor'd mother

" Enjoys the pleasures of the chase.

" Then banish Keppels and Sir Williams,

" Lady Babs and Lady Charlottes,

" Welcome gay pimps and bold postilions,

" And maudlin bawds and buxom harlots.

" No jealous eye our sports shall see;

" No tongue to tell, no pen to quote ;

" We'll take our pleasures lustily

" All sailing in the self-same boat."

D

CANVAS AFTER ELECTION.

" Put out the light and then——."
SHAKSPEARE.

IN *tented field,* our carpet knight

    Of warrior's blood ne'er shed a speck ;

He triumphs in a softer fight,

    And tilts upon the *tented deck !*

CANVAS AFTER ELECTION.

The grinning Pilot seems to mark
    That more is doing than he sees;
The crew's below; the tent is dark;
    Whose hand is that? whose feet are these?

The dullest mind can understand
    What of this scene must be the close,
If *that* be Baron Berghy's hand,
    And *these* the Queen of England's toes!

And tender accents strike the ear;
    " Ma vie, Mon cœur, most loved of men,
" Dismiss Majocci—banish fear
    " And O put out the light,—and then —"

THE BATH.

"————————— The wide sea

" Hath drops too few to wash her clean."

SHAKSPEARE.

THE weather's hot—the cabin's free!

And she's as free and hot as either!

And Berghy is as hot as she!

In short, they all are hot together!

THE BATH.

Bring then a large capacious tub,

    And pour great pails of water in,

In which the frowzy nymph may rub

    The itchings of her royal skin.

Let none but Berghy's hand untie

    The garter, or unlace the boddice;

Let none but Berghy's faithful eye

    Survey the beauties of the goddess.

While *she* receives the copious shower

    He gets a step in honour's path,

And grows from this auspicious hour

    A K-*night Companion of the Bath.*

JERUSALEM.

" Bear me to yon chamber ; there I'll lie,
" In that Jerusalem——"

SHAKSPEARE.

Riding on an ass a-straddle,
    Here the illustrious matron see,
Booted, on her Turkish saddle
    Smiling on her Bergami.

JERUSALEM.

Pray observe the Baron's bold eye,
  How with love it seems to hit her :
See his sister, Mrs. Oldi.
  Riding down hill in a litter.

English ships no longer tost in
  Hownam, Rollo, figure in,
Victorine and Billy Austin,
  Miss Dumont and Captain Flinn.

Here the crowd with jibes and jeerings
  Mark the Pilgrims as they pass,
Laugh at Bergy's ruff and ear-rings,
  And the Queen of England's Ass.

INNOCENT RECREATION.

" Wilt please you to see the *Bergamesque* dance !'
SHAKSPEARE.

MAHOMET behind the skreen
Gaily plies his merry work,
And our *very gracious* Queen
Gloats on the *Guoco* of the Turk.

INNOCENT RECREATION.

This *Guoco*, acted to the life
In luscious matter, very rich is—
One actor plays both man and wife,
And neither party wears the breeches.

Nor wine, nor ale, nor Mareschino,
Nor bath, nor ball, nor bower, nor bed,
Nor luscious tales of Mrs. Pino,
Could a more rapturous influence shed.

See how it works upon the set
Around, the hot contagion flies!
You think you see with Mahomét,
The *hoories* of his paradise.

E

HARMLESS AMUSEMENT.

" A bed, Iago, and not mean harm :
" It is hypocrisy against the Devil."

SHAKSPEARE.

HERE'S a pretty sight to gaze on,
    Such a story ne'er was read,
See the Lady with her stays on,
    Romping, rolling on the bed.

HARMLESS AMUSEMENT.

'Tis no " Custom of our Nation,"
   Which the artist strives to paint ;
Yet it seems some celebration
   In honor of our patron saint.

It is harmless recreation,
   Quite primæval in its kind,
And with a dame of reputation,
   Cannot leave a stain behind.

Therefore—Barb'ra Kress is perjured,
   For from what she twice repeats
It appears—but we've too much heard,—
   Vide evidence *in Sheets*.

ST. OMER'S.

"The exile of her minion is too new,
"She has not yet forgot him."

SHAKSPEARE.

Must she quit her whiskered beauty?
    Must she go with Matthew Wood?
Yes—he tells her, 'tis her duty,
    All for *his* and England's good.

ST. OMER'S.

Crazy Brougham, her fee'd adviser,
    Shakes his head with hums and haas,
Seems to think it would be wiser,
    If she tarried where she was.

Watch her look—then mark the carriage,
    Glittering with old England's arms,
Her's by suff'rance and by MARRIAGE,
    Giv'n to pay a lacquey's charms.

See the amorous matron barter,
    All for sport her worldly goods,
Quite resolved to cross the water,
    Just the thing for Mrs. Wood's!

CONSCIOUS INNOCENCE.

" With God, her conscience, and this bar against her."

SHAKSPEARE.

CONSCIENCE makes cowards of us all,

But this great dame grows daily bolder;

No fears her courage can appall,

She startles all who dare behold her.

CONSCIOUS INNOCENCE.

And as the moment yet draws nearer,

    She seems more hardened to the war,

Drinks more of Tyrwhitt's old Madeira,

    And draws still closer to the bar.

The doors unfold—and oh, what wonders!

    Majocci shows with his honest face,

"Wh at, Theodore there?" she loudly thunders,

    And rushes frantic from her place.

What moves her thus to quit her station,

    What drives th' Illustrious Matron hence?

CONSCIENCE itself makes proclamation,

    And thus declares her INNOCENCE!

THE END.

W. Shackell, Printer, Johnson's-court, Fleet-street, London.

NEW WORKS PUBLISHED THIS DAY,
BY W. WRIGHT, 46, FLEET-STREET.

Price 3s. boards.

1. **TENTAMEN ;** or, an Essay towards the History o Whittington, some time Lord Mayor of London. By VICESIMUS BLINKINSOP, L.L.D. F.R.S. A.S.S. &c. &c.

QUEEN'S TRIAL.—Nos. 1, to 12, price 7d. each, of

2. **THE QUEEN'S MAGAZINE.**—This Work will be exclusively dedicated to Her Majesty's Case ! The Numbers already published, contain a full Account of each day's proceedings in Parliament, upon the Bill of Pains and Penalties, illustrated with Documents connected with the subject.

" Look to the Queen."—SHAKSPEARE.

The Proprietors who have adopted the title of the Queen's Magazine, to distinguish it from the spurious publications of this trial, will feel themselves bound to publish each Number in rapid succession, so as to keep pace with the prcoeedings in the House of Lords.

3. **A CRITICAL EXAMINATION OF COBBETT'S** ENGLISH GRAMMAR, in a Letter to a Friend, shewing the Errors and Inconsistencies contained in that work, and the absurdity of the Author's proposed changes in the Established Grammatical Terms and Usages of the English Language. Price 1s. 6d.

4. **THE RADICAL LETTER BAG.** Correspondents :

Sir Jehu Face	-	A Radical	Mountebank,
Sir Whale Bones	-		Swiss Orator,
Sir Galen Gobble	-		Alchymist,
Sir Cordovan Bristlewood			Quidnunc.

By HUMPHREY MARTIAL. Price 2s.

5. *To Members of Parliament.*—**THE NEW WHIG** GUIDE, price 7s. 6d. boards, containing, the Choice of a Leader, Countess of Jersey's Masquerade, Change of Administration, important State Papers, Meeting at Burlington-house, Failure of the Buccaneers, and loss of the Broom fire-ship ; Trial of Henry Brougham for Mutiny, Methuen's support of Lord Althorp on the Leather Tax, extraordinary Parliamentary Debate, and other important articles.

6. **DR. SYNTAX IN PARIS**; or, A Tour in Search of the Grotesque, with 18 humourous Plates, price 1l. 1s. boards, or in Eight Parts, at 2s. 6d. each ; by the same Author who produced the original popular work.

7. **BEAUTIES OF THE MODERN POETS**, price 9s. boards, embellished with a beautiful Frontispiece ; being selections from the books of the most popular Authors of the present day, and an introductory View of the Modern Temple of Fame. By D. CAREY.

8. **NEW JOURNEY TO PERSIA**, price 12s. boards, with a large Map and elegant Plate, by a Persian Artist. A Narrative of a Journey into Persia, and Residence at Teheran, with a descriptive Itinerary from Constantinople to the Persian Capital ; also a variety of Anecdotes, illustrative of the inhabitants, religion, commerce, military poficy of the Government, &c. &c. from the French of M. Tancoigne, attached to the Embassy of General Gardane, with Notes and Observations. By E. BLAQUIERE, Esq. R.N., Author of Letters from the Mediterranean, &c. &c.

THE

POLITICAL SHOWMAN—AT HOME!

EXHIBITING HIS CABINET OF CURIOSITIES AND

Creatures—All Alive!

BY THE AUTHOR OF THE

POLITICAL HOUSE THAT JACK BUILT.

"I lighted on a certain place where was a *Den*."　　　*Bunyan.*

WITH TWENTY-FOUR CUTS.

"The putrid and mouldering carcase of exploded Legitimacy."
Mr. Lambton.

Second Edition.

LONDON:

PRINTED FOR WILLIAM HONE, 45, LUDGATE-HILL.

1821.

ONE SHILLING.

THE PRESS, invented much about the same time with the *Reformation*, hath done more mischief to the discipline of our Church, than all the doctrine can make amends for. 'Twas an happy time, when all learning was in manuscript, and some little officer did keep the keys of the library! Now, since PRINTING came into the world, such is the mischief, that *a man cannot write a book but presently he is answered!* There have been ways found out to *fine* not the people, but even the *grounds and fields where they assembled:* but no art yet could prevent these SEDITIOUS MEETINGS OF LETTERS! Two or three brawny fellows in a corner, with meer ink and elbow-grease, do more harm than an *hundred systematic divines.* Their ugly printing *letters,* that look but like so many rotten teeth, how oft have they been pulled out by the public tooth-drawers! And yet these rascally operators of the press have got a trick to fasten them again in a few minutes, that they grow as firm a set, and as biting and talkative as ever! O PRINTING! how hast thou *" disturbed the peace!"* Lead, when moulded into bullets, is not so mortal as when founded into *letters!* There was a mistake sure in the story of Cadmus; and the *serpent's teeth* which he sowed, were nothing else but the *letters* which he invented.

Marvell's Rehearsal transprosed, 4to, 1672.

Being marked only with *four and twenty letters,—variously transposed* by the help of a PRINTING PRESS,—PAPER works miracles. The Devil dares no more come near a *Stationer's* heap, or a *Printer's Office,* than *Rats* dare put their noses into a Cheesemonger's Shop.

A Whip for the Devil, 1669. p. 92.

THE SHOWMAN.

Ladies and Gentlemen,

Walk *up!* walk *up!* and see the Curiosities and

CREATURES—all alive! alive O! Walk *up!*—now's your time!—*only* a shilling. Please to walk *up!*

Here is the strangest and most wonderful *artificial* CABINET in Europe!—made of NOTHING—but *lacker'd brass, turnery,* and *papier mâché*—all FRET *work* and *varnish,* held together by *steel points!*—very CRAZY, but very CURIOUS!

Please to walk in, Ladies and Gentlemen—it's well worth *seeing!* Here are the most wonderful of all wonderful LIVING ANIMALS. Take care! Don't go within their *reach*— they mind nobody but *me!* A short time ago they got loose, and, with some other *vermin* that came from their *holes and corners,* desperately attacked a LADY OF QUALITY; but, as luck would have it, *I,* and *my 'four and twenty men,'* happened to come in at the very moment;—we ' *pull'd*' away, and prevented 'em from doing her a *serious mischief.* Though they *look tame,* their vicious dispositions are unchanged. If any thing was to happen to *me,* they'd soon break out *again,* and shew their natural ferocity. *I'm in continual danger from 'em myself*—for if I didn't watch 'em closely they'd *destroy* ME. As the clown says, ' there never *was* such times,'—so there's no telling what *tricks* they may play *yet.*

Ladies and Gentlemen,—these animals have been exhibited *at Court,* before the KING, and all the Royal Family! Indeed His Majesty is so *fond* of 'em that he often sees 'em *in private,* and *feeds* 'em; and he is so *diverted* by 'em that he has been pleased to express his gracious approbation of all their *motions.* But they're as cunning as the *old one* himself! Bless you, he does not know a thousandth part of their *tricks.* You, Ladies and Gentlemen, may see 'em just as they are!—the BEASTS and REPTILES—all *alive! alive* O! and the BIG BOOBY—all *a-light! a-light* O!

Walk in, Ladies and Gentlemen! walk in! just a-going to begin.——Stir 'em up! Stir 'em *up* there with *the long pole!*

Before I describe the ANIMALS, please to look at the SHOW-CLOTH opposite——— ☞

The CURIOSITIES have *labels* under them, which the company can *read.*

THE TRANSPARENCY, of which this is a copy, was exhibited by WILLIAM HONE, during the ILLUMINATION commencing on the 11th, and ending on the 15th of November, 1820, in celebration of the VICTORY *obtained by* THE PRESS *for the* LIBERTIES OF THE PEOPLE, which had been assailed in the Person of *The Queen* : the words "TRIUMPH OF THE PRESS," being displayed in variegated lamps as a motto above it. On the 29th, when *The Queen* went to St. Paul's, it was again exhibited, with Lord Bacon's immortal words, "KNOWLEDGE IS POWER," displayed in like manner.—The Transparency was painted by Mr. GEORGE CRUIKSHANK.

—————— COURT VERMIN that buzz round
And fly-blow the King's ear; make him suspect
His wisest, faithfullest, best counsellors—
Who, for themselves and their dependants, seize
All places, and all profits; and who wrest,
To their own ends, the statutes of the land,
Or safely break them. *Southey's Joan of Arc.* b. x.

¶ **Chese creaturis sece not to teche vs to corecte owr maners and amende our lyuynge.**
Dialoges of Creatures Moralysed. Prologe.

To exalt virtue, expose vice, promote truth, and help men to serious reflection, is my first moving cause and last directed end. *De Foe's Review,* 4to., 1705, Preface.

—————— Oh that I dared
To basket up the family of plagues
That waste our vitals; peculation, sale
Of honour, perjury, corruption, frauds
By forgery, by subterfuge of law,
By tricks and lies—————————
Then cast them, closely bundled, every brat
At the right door! *Cowper.*

NOTE.

All the Drawings are by Mr. GEORGE CRUIKSHANK.

"JUGLATOR REGIS."   *Strutt's Sports*, 188.

————————a most officious Drudge,
His face and gown drawn out with the same budge,
His pendant Pouch, which is both large and wide,
Looks like a *Letters*-patent:—————
He is as *awful*, as he had been sent
From Moses with the eleventh commandement.
                                Bp. Corbet's Poems, 1672, p. 3.

He is like a tight-rope dancer, who, whenever he leans on *one side*, counteracts his position
by a corresponding declination on *the other*, and, by this means, keeps himself in a most
self-satisfied equipoise.   *Retrospective Review*, No. V. p. 115.

Trust not the cunning waters of his eyes:—
His eyes drop millstones.   *Shakspeare.*

BAGS.—*(a Scruple Balance.)*

————— 'tis the veriest madness, to live poor,
And die with *Bags*——   *Gifford's Juvenal*, Sat. xiv.

DUBIUS is such a *scrupulous* good man—
Yes—you may catch him tripping, if you can!
He would not, with a PEREMPTORY tone,
Assert the nose upon his face HIS OWN
With HESITATION, admirably slow,
He humbly hopes—presumes—it MAY be so.
Through constant dread of giving truth offence,
He ties up all his hearers in SUSPENSE
His sole opinion, whatsoe'er befall,
Cent'ring, AT LAST, in having—NONE AT ALL.
                                        Cowper.

Well! he is a *nimble* gentleman; set him upon BANKES,
his horse, in a saddle rampant, and it is a great question, which
part of the Centaur shews better tricks.
                        Cleveland's Poems, 1665, p. 183.

By some the Crocodile is classed among fishes. A person born under this Zodiacal Sign, (*Pisces*), shall ' be a mocker and shall be *covetous*, he will *say* one thing and *doe* another, he shall *find money*, he will trust in his *supience*, and shall have *good fortune*, he shall be *a defender of Orphelins and widdowes* and shall live lxxiii year and v months after nature.'

Shepheard's Kalender, 1497. c. liii.

Pitty not him, but fear thyself,
Though thou see the crafty elfe
Tell down his silver-drops unto thee,
They're counterfit, and will undoe thee.   *Crashaw's Poems*, 1670, p. 112-

A CROCODILE.

LADIES AND GENTLEMEN,

     I begin the Exhibition with the Crocodile, which is of the Lizard tribe ; yet, from his *facility of creeping through narrow and intricate ways*, he has been classed among SER- PENTS.* He has a monstrous appetite, his *swallow* is immense, and his legs are placed *side*-ways. It is a vulgar error to suppose that he cannot *turn*; for, although he is in appearance very heavy, and his back very strong, and proof against the hardest blows, yet he is so *pliable*, that he can *wheel* round with the utmost facility. When in his HAUNT, and apparently torpid, he sometimes utters a piteous *whine* of distress—almost human; *sheds tears*, and, attracting the unwary, suddenly darts upon a man and gorges him with all he has. His *claws* are very long and tenacious. If a victim eludes his grasp, he infallibly secures him by his FLEET power. He is sometimes used for purposes of *state and show*, and his BAGS are much coveted for their *peculiar* qualities.†

    * By Linnæus.   † Goldsmith's Animated Nature, v. 283.

B

Above the steeple shines a plate,
That *turns, and turns,* to indicate
From what point blows the weather ;
Look up.——

Cowper.

Having by much dress, and secrecy, and dissimulation, as it were *periwigged** his sin, and covered his shame, he looks after no other innocence but *concealment.*

Bp. South's Sermons.

A MASK.——*(an Incrustation——a Relique.)*

A shallow brain behind a serious *mask,*
An oracle within an empty cask,
A solemn fop.———
——A sooty *Film.*

Cowper.

————————————————— The Thing on Earth
Least qualified in honour, learning, worth,
To occupy a sacred, awful post,
In which the best and worthiest tremble most.
The royal letters are a thing of course,
A King, that would, might recommend his horse;
And deans, no doubt, and chapters, with one voice,
As bound in duty, would confirm the choice.

*   *   *   *   *   *   *   *   *   *   *

A piece of mere Church-furniture at best.

Cowper.

* There is a similarity, amounting almost to absolute identity, in the two Greek words that signify an *Impostor* and *a Periwig:*—

Φεναξ-αχος—*Impostor.*

Φενάκη—*Periwig.*

Hederici Lexicon.

278

There are a number of us creep
Into this world, to eat and sleep;
And know no reason why they're born,
But merely to consume the corn.   *Watts* on *Hor.* L. i. Ep. ii. 27.

Very grievous were they; before them there were no such locusts as they, neither after them shall be such: for they covered the face of the whole earth, so that the land was *darkened*.
Exodus, x. 14, 15.

THE LOCUST.

LADIES AND GENTLEMEN,

The Locust is a destructive insect, of the GRILL US tribe. They are so numerous, and so rapacious, that they may be compared to an ARMY, pursuing its march to devour the fruits of the earth, as an instrument of *divine displeasure* towards a devoted country. They have LEADERS, who direct their motions in preying on the labours of man *in fertile regions*. No insect is more formidable in places where they breed: for they *wither* whatever they *touch*. It is impossible to recount the *terrible devastations* which historians and travellers relate that they have committed at different times, in various parts of the world. Many are so *venomous*, that persons *handling* them are immediately stung, and seized with shivering and trembling; but it has been discovered that, in most cases, their hateful qualities are completely assuaged by *palm* oil.*

* Goldsmith, vi. 21.

It preys upon and destroys itself with its own poison. It is of so malignant and ruinous a nature, that it ruins itself with the rest; and with rage mangles and tears itself to pieces.

Montaigne, v. 3. c. xi.

A SCORPION.

Ladies and Gentlemen,

The Scorpion is a REPTILE that resembles the *common lobster*, but is much more hideous.   They are very terrible to mankind, on account of their size and malignity, and their large *crooked stings*.   They often assault and kill people in their houses.   In ITALY, and some other parts of Europe, they are the greatest pests of mankind ; but their venom is most dreadful in the *East*.   An inferior species sally forth at certain seasons, in battalions ;—scale houses that stand in the way of their march ;—wind along the course of rivers ;—and on their retreat entrench themselves.   Scorpions are so irascible, that they will attempt to sting a *constable's staff ;* yet even a harmless little MOUSE* destroyed three of them, *one after the other*, by acting on the *defensive*, survived their venomous wounds, and seemed pleased with its victory. When in a confined space, they exert all their rage against each other, and there is nothing to be seen but universal carnage.   If this mutual destruction did not prevail, they would multiply so fast as to render some countries uninhabitable.†

* Confined for the sake of experiment in a vessel, by Maupertuis.   † Goldsmith, v. 428.

THE LOBSTER.

——————they preferre
Broiles before Rest, and place their Peace in Warre.   *Du Bartas*, 4to. 151.

LADIES AND GENTLEMEN,

The Lobster is very similar to the scorpion. It is *armed* with *two* great *claws*, by the help of which it moves itself *forwards*. They *entrench* themselves in places that can be easily defended where they acquire defensive and offensive *armour*. They issue forth from their *fortresses* in hope of *plunder*, and to surprise such inadvertent and weak animals as come within their reach. They have little to apprehend except from each other, the more powerful being formidable enemies to the weaker. They sometimes continue in the same habitations for a long time together; in general they get *new coats once a year*. When in *hot water* they make a great noise, attack any one that puts a hand towards them, and knowing their danger, use violent efforts to escape. In a sufficient heat they *change their colours*.*

* Goldsmith, v. 163.

———————— With huge fat places stored,
'A *prop* that helps to shoulder up the state.
Tom of Bedlam, folio. 1701. p. 4.

———————— a *Crutch* that helps the *weak* along,
Supports the *feeble*—but *retards the strong.*   *Smith.*

He knows not what it is to feel within
A comprehensive faculty, that grasps
Great purposes with ease, that turns and wields,
Almost without an effort, plans too vast
For his conception, which he cannot move.   *Cowper.*

One of that class of individuals of but moderate talents, who by habitual exercise of their faculties are enabled to figure in the world by mere *imitation;* to become learned moralists, jurists, and theologians; to go through the ceremonies of professional life with an imposing gravity and regularity, and to run round the mill-horse circle of routine with a scrupulous precision.
      Sir C. Morgan's Phil. of Life, 370

A *PRIME* CRUTCH.—

(From the Westminster Infirmary—Upper Ward).

HE fondly ' IMITATES' that wondrous LAD,
   That durst assay the sun's bright flaming team;
Spite of whose feeble hands, the horses mad
   Fling down on burning earth the scorching beam;—
     So MADE. *the flame in which* HIMSELF *was fired;*
     THE WORLD THE BONFIRE WAS—*when* HE *expired!**
     Like HIM of Ephesus, HE HAD WHAT HE DESIRED.
               Fletcher's Purple Island.

* The 'LAD' died in the midst of war, ejaculating heaven to save the country from the miseries of his system of misrule.

I don't think myself obliged to play tricks with my own neck, by putting it *under his feet*, to inform myself whether he wears sparrow-bills in his shoes or no.   *Asgill's Defence*, 1712, p. 15.

THE OPOSSUM.

LADIES AND GENTLEMEN,

This is a *quick climbing* animal; but is, in other respects, *heavy* and helpless. When it is pursued on *level ground* and overtaken, it feigns itself dead, to deceive the hunters. A faculty in its *seat*, enables it to suspend itself from a high branch, by that part, for a long time together; and, in this position, watching for whatever is weak that comes within its reach, it falls upon it and usually destroys it. By this elevating power in its *nether end*, it not only seizes its prey more securely, but preserves itself from pursuers; looking down on them, in a sort of *upright* position, heels upwards. It is very domesticated, but proves a disagreeable inmate, from its *scent*; which, however fragrant in *small* quantities, is uniformly ungrateful when *copiously* supplied. *It is a* BOROUGHING *creature.**

* Goldsmith, iii. 322. Stedman's Surinam. Shaw's Zoology.

Full of business, bustle, and chicanery;   *Dibdin's Bibl. Decam.* iii. 301.

An odious and vile kind of creatures that fly about the *House;*   *B. Jonson's Discov.*

> They seem—*descending,* at some direful blow,
> To *nibble brimstone* in the realms below!   *Salmagundi,* 139.

Suppose one to be " boring" on *one side* for two hours, and his opponent to be " bothering" for a like period on the *other side*, what must be the consequence?

Sir Jos. Yorke, in H. of Com. March 30, 1821.

> Of torrent tongue, and never blushing face;
> ———— Knaves, who, in truth's despite,
> Can white to black transform, and black to white!
>
> *Gifford's Juvenal,* Sat. iii.

When they were fewer, men might have had a Lordship safely conveyed to them in a piece of parchment no bigger than your hand, though several sheets will not do it safely in this wiser age.

Walton's Angler, (4to. Bagster) 93.

They'll argue as confidently as if they spoke gospel instead of law; they'll cite you six hundred several Precedents, though not one of them come near to the case in hand; they'll muster up the authority of Judgments, Deeds, Glosses, and Reports, and tumble over so many dusty Records, that they make their employ, though in itself easy, the greatest slavery imaginable; always accounting that the best plea which they have took most pains for.   *Erasmus of Folly,* 96.

In other countries, they make laws upon laws and add precepts upon precepts, till the endless number of them makes the fundamental part to be forgotten; leaving nothing but a confused heap of explanations, which may cause ignorant people to doubt whether there is really any thing meant by the laws or not.   *Bp. Berkeley's Gaudentio di Lucca,* 166.

In the country of the *Furr'd Law-cats,* they gripe all, devour all, conskite all, burn all, draw all, hang all, quarter all, behead all, murder all, imprison all, waste all, and ruin all, without the least notice of right or wrong: for among *them* vice is called virtue; wickedness, piety; treason, loyalty; robbery, justice: *Plunder* is their motto; *and all this they do, because they dare.* —*Gripe-men-all,* the *Chief* of the *Furr'd Law-cats,* said to Pantagruel. ' *Our* Laws are like cobwebs; your silly *little* flies are stopt, caught, and destroy'd therein, but your *stronger* ones break them, and force and carry them which way they please. Don't think we are so mad as to set up our nets to snap up your *great* Robbers and tyrants: no, *they* are somewhat too hard for us, there's no meddling with them; for they will make no more of *us,* than we make of the little ones.' —   *Rabelais,* b. v. c. xi, xii.

BLACK RATS.—*(Stuffed.)*

LADIES AND GENTLEMEN,

These are most pernicious animals. They BO-
ROUGH, and prey on our food, drink, clothing, furniture,
live-stock, and every convenience of life; furnishing their
residences with the plunder of our property. They have
particular HAUNTS, to which they entice each other in large
numbers, for the sake of *prey;* where they often do incredible damage to our *mounds,* and undermine the strongest
embankments. Sometimes they hoard their plunder in *nests,*
that they make at a distance from their usual *places of congre-
gating.** They are very bold and fierce. Instead of waiting
for an attack, they usually become the aggressors, and, *seizing
their adversaries by the lips,* inflict dangerous, and even deadly
wounds. While they subsist on our industry, and increase
our terrors, they make no grateful returns, and, therefore,
mankind have studied various ways for diminishing their
numbers; but their *cunning* discovers the most distant danger, and if any are disturbed or attacked, in an unusual manner, the rest take the alarm, and, becoming exceedingly shy,
and wary, elude the most ingenious devices of their pursuers.
When, unhappily, you come in contact with one of these
vermin, the best way of dispatching it is by a single squeeze;
but novices who hesitate, are sure to prove sufferers. They
have been found on a BENCH, so *interwoven* by their tails,
that *by reason of their entanglement, they could not part.†*
A DEAD RAT, *by altering the look of his* HEAD *and the appearance of his* SKIN, may be transformed into the appearance
of a much more *powerful* animal; and THIS, Ladies and
Gentlemen, *has been considered a* MASTER PIECE *in cheating.‡*

---

* White's Selborne, 4to. 75.   † Letters from Bodleian Library, i. 12.
‡ Ibid.ii. 160, *note.* See also Goldsmith, iii. 169.

A *bait,* such wretches to beguile.   *Spenser.*

C

Cadger. *n. s.* A *Low* Character. *Pierce Egan.*

One of
" The blessings of this *most indebted* land."

* * *

Useless in him alike both brain and speech,
Fate having plac'd all truth above his reach. *Cowper.*

A most damnable swearer and inventor of new oaths. A tongue-libelling lad of the sea—he matters not the truth of any thing he speaks; but is prone to fasten his stings in the reputation of those that would scorn to be like him. I wonder to see this unquiet disposition in a brute creature—a Swill-tub. *Pell's Improvement of the Sea,* 1695, p. 101, *et seq.*

A *CADGE* ANCHOR.—*(a Remora— a sucking Fish.)*

WHAT have we here? a man or a fish? A FISH: he *smells* like a fish; a very *ancient* and fish-like smell; a kind of, not of the newest, Poor John. Were I in England now (as once I was) and had but this fish painted, not a holiday fool there but would give a piece of silver : *there* would this monster make a man; any *strange beast* there makes a man. His gabbling voice is to utter FOUL SPEECHES, and to DE-TRACT. He is as disproportioned in his manners, as in his shape. As with age his body grows uglier, his mind cankers.
CALIBAN.

Reptil, with spawn abundant—   *Milton, Par. L.* b. 7.

A WATER SCORPION.

Ladies and Gentlemen,

      This offensive insect lives in *stagnant* waters, continually watching for prey. Its feelers resemble the claws *of* a scorpion; the eyes are *hard and prominent*, the shoulders *broad and flat.* It wastes twenty times as much as its appetite requires; one can destroy thirty or forty of the libellula kind, each as large as itself. It is nevertheless greatly overrun with a small kind of lice, which probably repay the injuries it inflicts elsewhere. At certain seasons it flies to *distant waters* in search of food; but it remains where it was produced until fully grown, when *it sallies forth in search of a companion of the other sex, and soon begets an useless generation.**

    * Martyn's Dict. Nat. Hist. 2 vols. Folio, 1785.   Goldsmith, vi. 35.

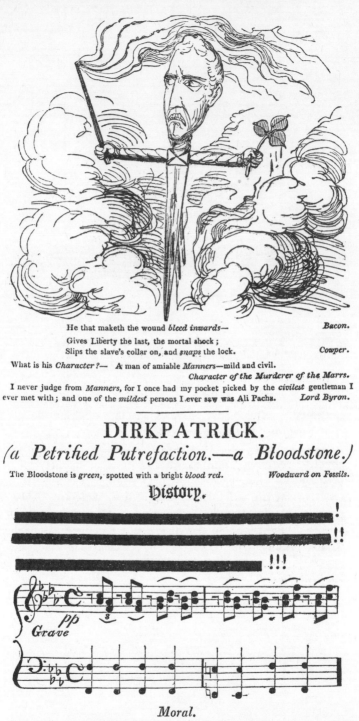

He that maketh the wound *bleed inwards*—   *Bacon.*

Gives Liberty the last, the mortal shock;
Slips the slave's collar on, and *snaps* the lock.   *Cowper.*

What is his *Character?*— A man of amiable *Manners*—mild and civil.
      Character of the Murderer of the Marrs.

I never judge from *Manners*, for I once had my pocket picked by the *civilest* gentleman I ever met with; and one of the *mildest* persons I ever saw was Ali Pacha.   *Lord Byron.*

DIRKPATRICK.

(a Petrified Putrefaction.—a Bloodstone.)

The Bloodstone is *green*, spotted with a bright *blood red.*   *Woodward on Fossils.*

𝕳istory.

Moral.

I recommend it to all that read this *History*, that when they find their lives come up, in any degree, to a similitude of cases, they will inquire and ask themselves, is not this the time to repent?   *De Foe's Col. Jack*, 1723, p. 399.

——————— *Raised* in blood. Shakspeare.

THE BLOODHOUND.

LADIES AND GENTLEMEN,

This is the most terrible animal in the Collection. Its character is that of decided *enmity to man;* it hunts down those who endeavor to regain their *Liberty,* and is called the *Ban* Dog. When it scents a human victim it follows his track with cruel perseverance, flies upon him with dreadful ferocity, and, unless dragged off, tears and rends the form until every noble feature of humanity is destroyed. It has an exquisite smell for blood. The species vary little throughout the world : there is scarcely any difference between the trans-atlantic *Spanish* blood-hound and the *Irish* wolf-dog, whose ferocity has been much diminished by the animal being frequently *crossed.* It is still kept on some of the old *royal grounds.*

* Edwards's West Indies. Goldsmith. Rainsford's St. Domingo. Scott's Sportsman's Repository.

I do remember an APOTHECARY—
    A THREE-INCH FOOL ;—*unmannerly breech'd* :—   *Shakspeare.*
    Inflated and astrut with self-conceit :—   *Cowper.*
To *bleed* adventured he not, *except the Poor.*   *Swift's Mem. of P. P.*
    He had heard of *Politics*, and long'd to get
    A *Place ;* ——————————— and now,
    With *all his Fam'ly* crowding at his heels,
    His brothers, cousins, followers, and his son,
    He shows himself *Prime Doctor.*—   *Rt. Hon. G. Canning.*
      He is that CANTING SLAVE foretold,
      By one Dan Barnaby of old,
      That would hang up his cat on Monday,
      For killing of a mouse on Sunday ;
      Who, that *his* beer mayn't work the latter day,
      Forbids the brewer's call on Saturday.   *Anon.*
A *go-cart* of superstition and prejudice, never stirring hand or foot but as he is pulled by the
wires and strings of the state conjurers.   *Hazlitt's Table Talk,* 366.
His A. B. C. is a great deal better employment for him, than the grave and weighty matters
of state, and the study of politics.   *Dr. Bastwick against Col. J. Lilburne,* 42.
Shall I lose my *Doctor ?* No ; he gives me the potions, and the *motions.*
    What ho ! APOTHECARY !——   *Shakspeare.*

THE DOCTOR.—*(a Dejection.)*

In these days the grand *"primum mobile"* of England is CANT—*Cant political, Cant religious,
Cant moral,* but *always* CANT—a thing of words, without the smallest influence upon actions;
the English being no wiser, no better, and much poorer, and more divided among themselves, as
well as far less moral, than they were before the prevalence of this *Verbal Decorum.*
    Lord Byron on Mr. Bowles, 16.

DIARY.—April 1st. I grew *melancholy*.—My father lying
sick, told me, in syllables, the *Philosopher's stone.*—It pleased
God to put me in mind that I was now placed in the condition
I always desired.—I hung three spiders about my neck *(for
a charm)*.—I kissed the king's hand.—*Cœtera desunt.*
    Elias Ashmole's Diary.

—————— the most notorious geck and *Gull*
That e'er Invention play'd on.

Shakspeare.

THE BOOBY.

LADIES AND GENTLEMEN,

The *Creature* you now see is a sort of *Noddy* of the GULL kind. Observe his uncouth form and his ludicrously wise looks! He is the most stupid of the *feathered* tribe; yet he has a *voracious* appetite, and an enormous swallow. You perceive that he feigns the appearance of being *upright*, of seeming to comprehend objects he sees, of listening to what he hears, and that he shakes his head with *gravity*, as though he had a certain degree of understanding. His greatest pleasure is in *standing still*. He has not sense enough to *get out of People's way;* speaking to him or making *motions* never disturb him. There is no compelling him to the fatigue of *changing* his position till he feels a *blow;* for he keeps his PLACE till he is approached quite close, and *knocked down*. He is a living *full stop*. When he is *forced to walk*, which is very seldom, he goes from *side to side*. Like others of similar tribes, he BOROUGHS. In this respect the union and affection of these *Creatures* towards each other is wonderful; for, when undisturbed by the encroachments of *men*, they construct their *nests* as convenient as if they expected them to be *permanent;* arranging their different PLACES with such an amazing degree of uniformity, as to resemble a *regular plantation*. Sometimes they draw up side by side, in rank and file, and sit brooding together as if in deep counsel, on affairs of moment—their *silliness* and *solemnity* exciting involuntary *laughter!* This *burlesque* takes place, in particular,

about the month of *November*. The habits of these tribes
are known through those who visit the haunts they have forsaken for more obscure *retreats*, where they can *build aloft*,
and settle in their *nests* at ease : a practice which confirms the
remark of a great naturalist, that the presence of *men* not only
destroys the society of the *meaner* animals, but even extin-
guishes their *grovelling* instincts. Hitherto the Booby has
been considered of no service whatever; yet a similar species,*
by drawing a wick through the body and lighting it, is made
into a *candle*.† If this Booby could be thus used, the *illumination of* BOTH HOUSES *and the* PUBLIC OFFICES might
be speedily effected, and the tribe he belongs to be rendered
available to human purposes. At any rate a skilful tallow-
chandler might try his hand at converting the *Creature* into

A TWOPENNY FLAT

FOR A COBBLER'S STALL;

——————— which, with short cotton wicks,
Touch'd by *th' industr'ous Cob's* Promethean art,.
Starts into light—and makes the lighter start !   *Rejected Addresses.*

* Mother Carey's Chickens—the *Peterel.*   † Martyn. Bewick.

The Creature's at his *dirty* work again.   *Pope.*

THE SLOP PAIL.

LADIES AND GENTLEMEN,

THE " SLOP PAIL" being occupied by " SLOP"
keeping his *tri-colored* cockade in it, with the hope of bleach-
ing it *white*, has become more and more offensive daily, and
will be *kicked down.**

---

* So ' the Jacobite Relics of Scotland' *fall low*,
  When MENDACITY HOGG dares *his betters* to brow,
  And turns up *HIS* SNOUT, with derision and scorn,
  At those, who, *less cringing*, to labor are born:—
  The *parasite* pride of his *mendicant* mind
  Pimps himself " to bewilder, and dazzles to blind;"
  Yet I still wish him well—for I wish that he may
  Learn, that wrong can't be right, and—be *honest* as they.

                    See Dedication of *Hogg's Jacobite Relics,*
                        to the Highland Society of London.

D

The GREAT BOOTS having been *out of order*, were *welted*, and afterwards new *vamped*, and *polished*. Dr. SOUTHEY, *the Varnisher*, has them in hand at present, and is ' *doing them up*' as fast as possible.

LADIES AND GENTLEMEN,

I thank you for your company. Opposite to you is a description of THE MONSTER that my people are now *hunting* on the Continent. When *destroyed*, its skin will be stuffed and preserved among the other Antiquities and Curiosities in the *European Museum.*

LADIES AND GENTLEMEN, I wish you *a good day.*— *Keep to* THE RIGHT. Walk *steadily* FORWARD. The *Animals* may make an *uproar*, but don't be alarmed; I'll see you safe OUT. Remember they are *under my control*, and cannot take a step beyond the reach of

MY EYE

I'll watch them *tame.*   *Shakspeare.*

BOA DESOLATOR,

OR

LEGITIMATE VAMPIRE.

It overlays the continent like an ugly Incubus, sucking the blood and stopping up the breath of man's life. It claims Mankind as its property, and allows human nature to exist only upon sufferance; it haunts the understanding like a frightful spectre, and oppresses the very air with a weight that is not to be borne. *Hazlitt's Political Essays and Characters*, p. 91.

THIS hideous BEAST, not having at any time put forth all his *members*, cannot be accurately described. Every *dark* Century has added to his frightful bulk. More disgusting than the filthiest reptile, his strength exceeds all other *brute force.*

His enormous, bloated, toad-like body is *ferruginous :** the under surface appears of *polished steel.*† His cavern-like mouth is always open to devour; ' his teeth are as *swords*, and his jaw-teeth as knives'—as millions of *bristling bayonets* intermingled with *black fangs* containing mortal venom. His roar is a voice from the sepulchre. He is marked ' *in form of a cross*,'‡ with a series of *chains*, intersected by the TRIANGLE,§ and glittering colours, variegated with *red*.

His aspect is cruel and terrible. He loves the *dark*, but never sleeps. Wherever he makes his lair, nature sickens, and man is brutified. His presence is ' plague, pestilence, and famine, battle, and murder, and sudden death.' His bite rapidly *undermines the strongest* CONSTITUTION, and dissolves the whole into an entire mass of CORRUPTION. He has no *brain*, but the *walls* of the skull emit a *tinkling* sound, that attracts his victims, and lulls them into *passive obedience*. In this state he clutches them in his coils, and *screws* and *squeezes* them to destruction—*slavering* them over, and sucking in their *substance* at leisure. It is difficult to witness the half-stifled cries of his harmless prey, or to behold its anxiety and trepidation, while the monster writhes hideously around it, without imagining *what our own case would be in the same dreadful situation.*‖

His rapacity is increased by *indulgence*. He grinds, cranches, and devours whole multitudes without being satisfied. His blood is cold. His ravening maw does not digest : it is an ever-yawning grave that *engulphs*—a ' bottomless pit' continually crying ' *give, give !*' Sometimes he

---

* Shaw's Zoology. Art. Boa, iii. 344.   † Ibid. 366.
‡ Linnæus's Nat. Hist. by Gmelin, 8vo. (Jones) 1816. Art. Boa Constrictor, xii. 437.
§ Shaw's Zoology, iii. 339.   ‖ Macleod's Wreck of the Alceste, 291, 295.

'rests from his labors,' to admire his loathsome *limbs*, and *slime* them over. He has no affections : yet he appears charmed by the *hum* of the INSECTS that follow him, and pleased by the *tickling crawl* of the MEANEST REPTILES—permitting them to hang upon his lips and partake of his leavings. But his real pleasure is in listening to the cries of his captives, the wail of the broken hearted, and the groans of the dying.

He lives in defiance and scorn of Providence, and in hatred to the happiness of man. When distended with human carnage, and wet with the gore of the innocent and the helpless, he lifts an impious *form* to heaven in solemn mockery. He was predicted of by the Seer of old, as the BEAST with many heads and crowns, bearing the name of BLASPHEMY.

The garish *colours* that denote his malignity, excite only horror and detestation in the lover of nature, and of his species. They are most *lively* when he is engaged in the work of death, and cause him to be admired by the vulgar multitude, learned and unlearned, who hold him *sacred*, pay him *divine honors*, call him *holy*, and fall down before him as an object of worship, while priests glorify him, and minister to him, and pray for his murderous successes in the temples. Hence the good and the wise, in all ages, have devised and practised various methods for the destruction of a FIEND that creates nothing but *terror* and *imposture*, and between whom and rational man there is a natural antipathy.

He is filled with the deadliest rage by the encreasing growth of the *pop'lar* TREE :—

> THAT TREE, beneath whose shade the Sons of Men
> Shall pitch their tents in peace.
> ————BRISSOT murder'd, and the blameless wife
> Of ROLAND! Martyr'd patriots, spirits pure,
> Wept by the good, ye fell! Yet still survives,
> Sown by your toil, and by your blood manured,
> The imperishable TREE ; and still its roots
> Spread, and strike deep.————
> *Southey's Joan of Arc*, b. iii.

His existence is drawing to a close. It has been ascertained that the way of putting him *quietly* out of the world is by a 𝔅𝔩𝔞𝔠𝔨 𝔇𝔬𝔰𝔢 consisting of the *four and twenty letters* * of the alphabet, properly *composed*, made up in certain *forms*, covered with sheets of white *paper*, and well *worked* in a *Columbian* PRESS. These PAPERS are to be *forced down his*

---

* Philostratus relates that the Indians destroy the most monstrous serpent by spreading *golden* LETTERS, *on a field of* RED, before his hole. They dazzle and confound him, and he is taken without difficulty.

throat DAILY, *morning and evening,* and on every *seventh* day a *double* dose should be administered. The operation is accelerated by the powerful *exhibition* of the WOOD DRAUGHTS. In a short time his *teeth* will fall out—he will be seized with catalepsy—in the last stage of MORTIFICATION, *he will* STING HIMSELF *to death;*—and all mankind, relieved from the deadened atmosphere under which they had been *gasping,* will make the first use of their *recovered breath,* to raise an universal shout of joy at the extinction of

THE LEGITIMATE VAMPIRE.

Those Lords of pray'r and prey—that *band* of Kings,
That Royal, rav'ning BEAST, whose vampire wings
O'er sleeping Europe treacherously brood,
And fan her into dreams of *promis'd* good,
Of Hope, of Freedom—but to drain her blood!   *Moore.*

THE END.   297

CATALOGUE

OF

WILLIAM HONE'S PUBLICATIONS.

₊ Some of the Works in this Catalogue are nearly out of Print, and
WILL NOT BE REPRINTED.

New Editions

OF THE

WOOD CUT WORKS.

One Shilling each.

1. POLITICAL HOUSE THAT JACK BUILT, 13 Cuts.
2. MAN IN THE MOON, 15 Cuts.
3. QUEEN'S MATRIMONIAL LADDER, 18 Cuts.

NON MI RICORDO! 3 Cuts—6d.

All the Drawings are
BY MR. GEORGE CRUIKSHANK.

₊ Fine Editions *Colored,* of the ' House that Jack built,' and the ' Matrimonial Ladder,' *Price* 3s.—The ' Man in the Moon,' 2s.—' Non mi Ricordo!' 1s.

With a Cut—Price 1s. 6d.

THE SPIRIT
OF DESPOTISM.

₊ The *Rare and Extraordinary Book,* bearing the above title, was *privately printed* without the name of printer or bookseller, and so effectually SUPPRESSED, that there are only *two* copies of it besides my own in existence.—Its real value consists in exhibiting an entire and luminous view of the causes and consequences of Despotic Power. Its enthusiastic and glowing Love of Liberty is unexcelled by any work written since; and for clearness, richness, and beauty of style, it is *Superior to every Production of the Press* within the same period. All that the author touches he turns into gold. I regret to say, that probably I shall never be at liberty to disclose his name. Naturally desirous that such a work should be perused by all England, *I have reprinted it verbatim* from my own Copy; and, (although containing as much in quantity as a volume of Gibbon's History of Rome,) it is sold for *Eighteen-pence.*
45, *Ludgate-Hill.*   WILLIAM HONE.
₊ The French, instantly perceiving the transcendent merit of the work, and its high importance at this crisis, have translated it, and it is now read throughout France with the greatest avidity.
N. B. *A large Paper* Edition. Price 3s. 6d. in bds.

Price 1s.— *With 2 Cuts.*

THE RIGHT DIVINE OF KINGS
TO GOVERN WRONG!

A Satire—with Notes, By the Author of the Political House that Jack Built.
₊ A large Paper Edition. Price 1s. 6d.

1. The Dropt Clauses out of the Bill against the Queen. For Mr. Attorney General to peruse and settle. With a Refresher, 6d.
2. The Queen's Letter to the King, 6d.
3. The Ghost of Chatham; a Vision. Dedicated to the House of Peers, 6d.
4. A Speech at Dublin, in behalf of the Queen. By JOHN FINLAY, Esq. Barrister at Law, 6d.
`5. The Form of Prayer, with Thanksgiving, for the happy Deliverance of her Majesty. With a *Cut,* 6d.

Price 1s.
A Full Report of

THE TRIAL
THE KING v. JOHN HUNT.

IN THE KING'S BENCH, FEBRUARY 21, 1821.
For a Libel on the House of Commons in
THE EXAMINER.
With a PREFACE, being an Answer to the Attorney General's Reply
BY THE SON OF THE DEFENDANT.
₊ The Trial contains Mr. JOHN HUNT'S most able DEFENCE VERBATIM, as I heard him make it *in person,* contending for the right of telling the plain Truth to his Countrymen. The Preface by Mr. John Hunt's *Son,* is animated by the Spirit of his noble-minded father.   W. HONE.

Price 1s. 6d.

THE RIGHT ASSUMED BY THE
JUDGES TO FINE A DEFENDANT,

While making his Defence in Person, *Denied :* being a Short-hand Report of the important Legal Argument of HENRY COOPER, Esq. Barrister at Law, in the *King* v. *Davison,* on moving for a New Trial:
WITH A PREFACE.

Price 1s.

TO THE KING.

From the Author of " *The King's Treatment of the Queen.*" (A most able Pamphlet).
" It is the curse of Kings to be attended by slaves that take their humours for a warrant."—*King John,*

Price 1s.

THE KING'S TREATMENT OF
THE QUEEN.

Price 2s.

THE PREROGATIVES OF A QUEEN
CONSORT OF ENGLAND.

Particularly of her ability to make and receive Gifts—to sue and be sued—to hold Courts without the King—its being Treason to plot against her Life—the modes of trying her for Offences—her ancient Revenue of Queen-Gold, &c. &c. *Only a few unsold.*

Price 1s.

THE QUEEN'S CASE STATED.
By CHARLES PHILLIPS, Esq.

Price 1s.

THE LAMENT OF THE EMER-
ALD ISLE,

On the DEATH of the Princess CHARLOTTE.
By CHARLES PHILLIPS, Esq.

Price 1s. 6d.

CAROLINE: A POEM.

" This is a Poem for the People, and contains some of those great truths which cannot be studied too much."—*Monthly Magazine, August.*

Price 4s. *in Boards.*

SPEECHES.

By CHARLES PHILLIPS, Esq.
Collected into one Volume.

In 8vo. 9th Edition, 1s.—(Color'd, 1s. 6d.)

THE ORIGIN OF
DOCTOR SLOP'S NAME.

By the Author of the House that Jack Built.

Price 1s.—India Proofs, 3s.

THE PORTRAITS OF QUIROGA, RIEGO, AGUERO, AND BANOS,

The Four distinguished FOUNDERS OF THE SPANISH REVOLUTION; which, on the 1st of January, 1820, they courageously commenced in Arms; and, to their immortal glory, secured, without bloodshed, by putting the law above the King.

Price 1s.

A BANK NOTE, NOT TO BE IMITATED!

With the *Bank Restriction Barometer,* or Scale of Effects on Society, of the Bank-note System and PAYMENTS IN GOLD.

*** "This Bank-note is by Mr. HONE, and ought to make the hearts of the Bank Directors (if they have hearts) ache at the sight."—*Examiner.*

In a large Octavo Volume, (containing nearly 700 pages), with an accurate Plan of St. Peter's Field, price 12s. in boards.

THE WHOLE PROCEEDINGS

before the

CORONER'S INQUEST AT OLDHAM,
&c.

On the Body of JOHN LEES,

Who died of Sabre Wounds received at MANCHESTER, August 16, 1819;

Being the fullest and only Authentic Information concerning the Transactions of that fatal Day; detailing the Evidence on both sides, *upon Oath;* the Legal Arguments before the Coroner; his various Decisions; the Application to the Court of King's Bench for a Mandamus to him to proceed; the Affidavits thereon; and the Petition of the Father of the Deceased to Parliament; with References to the Cases on the Subject, and a copious Analytical Index. Taken in Short-hand, and edited by J. A. DOWLING, Esq.

Price 2s.

REPORT OF THE MANCHESTER COMMITTEE. With the NAMES OF THE SUFFERERS, *(in the whole upwards of 600 killed and wounded;)* the nature and extent of their Injuries—an Account of the Distribution of the Funds, &c. Published by Order of the Committee.

In 1 Vol. 8vo. Price 4s. 6d. Boards.

THE EMIGRANT'S GUIDE TO THE UNITED STATES OF AMERICA:

By ROBERT HOLDITCH, Esq. of the Royal College of Surgeons.

Price 2s. 6d.

THE TRIAL OF ELIZ. FENNING,

Charged with administering Poison with intent to Murder. Printed verbatim from the Notes of the late Mr. SIBLY. With Notes and Illustrations; and some Account of the Sufferer and her Parents.

In one vol. 8vo. Price 9s. boards.

MYSTERIOUS CASE OF
ELIZABETH FENNING:

Being a Detail of extraordinary Facts discovered since her Execution, including the preceding *Report* of her singular TRIAL. Also, numerous Authentic Documents; and Strictures, By JOHN WATKINS, LL. D. With Thirty original Letters, written by the unfortunate Girl until she was put to Death.

Price 3s. 6d.

THOUGHTS ON THE FUNDING AND PAPER SYSTEM,

By N. J. DENISON, Esq.

MR. PHILLIPS'S SPEECHES.
(Sixpence each) viz.

Guthrie *v.* Sterne, (Adultery.)
O'Mullan *v.* M'Korkill, (Defamation).
Connaghtan *v.* Dillon, (Seduction).
Creighton *v.* Townsend, (Seduction).
Blake *v.* Wilkins, (Breach of Promise).
Browne *v.* Blake, (Adultery).
On the Catholic Question.
Character of Napoleon.
On the Dethronement of Napoleon, (at Liverpool).
First Letter to the Editor of the Edinburgh Review.
Second Letter to Ditto.
*** The Speeches may be had separate as above, or collected into one Volume—Price 4s. in boards.

In 1 Vol. 8vo. (630 Pages) 8s. in Boards.

THE REFORMISTS' REGISTER.
By WILLIAM HONE.

*** Only a few Copies of this Work remain unsold.

VARIOUS.

The Trials of the Blood Money Men in 1816. 2s. 6d.
The History of the Blood Conspiracy in 1756. 1s.
Trial.—Wright *v.* Braham, (Crim. Con.) 2s.
The Minister and the Mayor: A Poem, on Lord Sidmouth refusing to let Mr. Alderman Wood, when Lord Mayor, ride in State through Westminster, 1s.
The Midnight Intruder; or, Old Nick at C——n H——e. A Poem. By W. R. H. 1s. 6d.
Official Account of the Noble Lord's Bite, 4d.
Conrad the Corsair: a Tale, 4d.
All Lord Byron's Poems on his Domestic Circumstances, 23rd Edition, 1s.
Account of Napoleon's Deportation.

SIXPENCE EACH.

Lines on the Death of——. By *Thomas Moore, Esq.*
The undeniable Skill between Gammon the Black and Dandy Grey Russett, (coloured, 1s.)
Napoleon and the Bourbons.
French Principles.
Poetical Address to Lord Byron by Mrs. Henry Rolls.
The Regent's Bomb, with Illustrations in Prose and Verse; and a coloured CUT.
The Yacht for the Regent's Bomb. A Poetical Epistle, *with a coloured Cut.*
The Appearance of an Apparition to James Sympson, commanding him to do strange things in Pall Mall, and what he did, *with a coloured Cut.*
The Cruelties of the Algerine Pirates. Very interesting. *With an Engraving.*
THINGS NOT LIKELY TO HAPPEN, a Political Droll in Six Compartments, (lines and dots).

Colored Caricatures
BY MR. GEORGE CRUIKSHANK.

1. THE ROYAL SHAMBLES; or the Progress of Legitimacy, and Re-establishment of Religion and Social Order. On a Plate 22 inches wide, 3s.
2. BAGS NODLE'S FEAST; a New Ballad, founded on Fact—with *two* illustrative Caricatures, 2s.
3. LOUIS XVIII. *Climbing the Mat de Cocagne,* or Soaped Pole, to bear off the Imperial Crown, 2s.
4. FAST COLOURS—*Patience on a Monument smiling at Grief,* or the Royal Laundress washing Boney's Court Dresses, 1s.

Portraits
ONE SHILLING EACH.

1. LORD BYRON.
2. SIR ROBERT WILSON.
3. ELIZABETH FENNING.
4. WILLIAM NORRIS, an Insane American, *riveted alive in Iron,* and many Years confined, in that state, in a Cell in BETHLEM.—Sketched from the Life, in Bethlem, *(as he was seen there in 1815 by W. Hone,)* and etched by *G. Cruikshank.*
5. NAPOLEON, after David's original Picture, exhibited in London. A very good Portrait.
6. Nuptial Portraits of the Princess Charlotte and Prince Leopold, (Proofs, 2s.)
7. Napoleon on his abolishing the Slave Trade (a coloured Print with Letter-Press)—curious.

New Edition—enlarged.

In Octavo, Price 6s. in Boards.

THE APOCRYPHAL NEW TESTAMENT.

Being all the Gospels, Epistles, and other pieces now extant, attributed in the first four centuries to JESUS CHRIST, his Apostles, and their Companions, and not included in the New Testament, by its compilers. Translated and now first collected into One Volume. With Prefaces and Tables, and various Notes and References.

Question.

After the writings contained in the New Testament were selected from the numerous Gospels and Epistles then in Existence, what became of the Books that were rejected by the compilers?

Answer.

In the present Work the translations of all the rejected Books now in existence, are carefully collected, and a table of all that are lost is subjoined. He, therefore, who possesses the *New Testament* itself, and the *Apocryphal New Testament*, has, in the two volumes, a collection of all the Historical Records relative to Christ and his Apostles, now in existence, that were considered sacred by any sect of Christians during the first four centuries after his birth.

*** *Although the* Apocryphal New Testament *was put forth without pretension or ostentatious announcement, or even ordinary solicitude for its fate, yet a large Edition has been sold in a few Months. To this NEW EDITION there are some additions. There is annexed to it a Table of the years wherein all the Books of the ' New Testament' are stated to have been written ; to the Order of the Books of the ' Apocryphal New Testament' the AUTHORITIES from whence they have been taken are affixed ; and finally many errors have been corrected.*

A PROSPECTUS containing the *Additions* to complete the first Edition, and for the information of Inquirers respecting the work, may be had Price 6d.

In Foolscap, 8vo. Price 6s.

SIXTY CURIOUS AND AUTHENTIC NARRATIVES AND ANECDOTES

Respecting Extraordinary Characters; Illustrative of the tendency of Credulity and Fanaticism; exemplifying the Imperfections of Circumstantial Evidence; and recording singular instances of voluntary Human Suffering, and Interesting Occurrences. By JOHN CECIL, Esq. *With an Historical Plate.*

This most interesting little volume is so entertaining and select, in its facts and language, as to render it a very agreeable companion, and an acceptable present.

A Pocket Volume, Price 5s.

THE PICTURE OF THE PALAIS ROYAL:

Describing its Spectacles, Gaming-houses, Coffee-houses, Restaurateurs, Tabagies, Reading-rooms, Milliners'shops, Gamesters, Sharpers, Mouchards, Artistes, Epicures, Courtesans, Filles, and other Remarkable Objects in that High Change of the Fashionable Dissipation and Vice of Paris. With Characteristic Sketches, and Anecdotes of its Frequenters and Inhabitants. *With a large folding Coloured Engraving.* Visitors to Paris should take this work as a Guide and Mentor. Those who stay at hometwill be exceedingly amused by the singularity of manners it discloses.

In one Plate, Price 2s., India Proofs 4s.

AUTHENTIC PORTRAITS OF LAVALETTE, NEY, AND LABEDOYERE,

This Print was suppressed at Paris as soon as published.

MR. HAZLITT'S POLITICAL ESSAYS.

In 8vo. Price 14s. in Boards.

POLITICAL ESSAYS;

with Sketches of

PUBLIC CHARACTERS.

By WILLIAM HAZLITT.

CONTENTS—Dedication—Preface—Marquis Wellesley—Mr. Southey and his Lays—Dottrel-catching.—The Bourbons and Buonaparte—Vetus—The late War—Prince Maurice's Parrot—Congress.—Mr. Owen's New View—Mr. Western and Mr. Brougham—The Distresses of the Country—Mr. Coleridge and his Sermons—Buonaparte and Muller—Macirone and the Death of Murat—Wat Tyler—The Quarterly—The Courier—Dr. Slop—The Spy System—State Prisoners—Effects of War and Taxes—Court Influence—The Clerical Character—The Regal Character—Characters of Lord Chatham—Mr. Burke—Mr. Fox—Mr. Pitt—Examination of Mr. Malthus's Doctrines on Population, &c.—A Parallel between Mr. Pitt and Buonaparte, written by Mr. Coleridge, &c. &c.

*** *No man has lashed political apostacy with more severity, nor given harder blows to tyranny and tyrants of all kinds, than MR. HAZLITT. His literary excellencies are unsurpassed by any living writer ; especially in the just conception and masterly delineation of character. His volume is a Political Jewel House.*

In One Volume 8vo. Price 8s. in Boards.

POLITICAL SERMONS TO ASSES.

By the late JAMES MURRAY.

With a Memoir of the Author, and his Portrait.

*** I know not what to say more in praise of this Work, than that the pieces it contains, have been subjects of my reading and admiration from boyhood. Many of them were very scarce. During several years of diligent research I collected them with difficulty, and have reprinted the whole at a reasonable price. Civil and religious intolerance were never more successfully exposed, than by their close reasoning, and sarcastic irony. They abound with wit and humor, and the severest invectives of honest hearted patriotism.

W. HONE.

In One Volume 8vo. Price 8s.

THE SPEECHES

Of the Right Hon. J. P. CURRAN.

A NEW AND ENLARGED COLLECTION.

With Memoirs of Mr. Curran, and his *Portrait.*

*** Eloquence has perhaps never suffered a deeper loss than by the imperfect manner in which the Speeches of this immortal Orator have been collected. The present edition embodies his relics, and contains *seven full speeches, with two extracts, in no other Collection.* These grand efforts of oratorical genius leave the reader's mind in awful astonishment at the daring honesty of the intrepid advocate, and disclose scenes, wherein the majestic figure of the Patriot rose in sublime and solitary pre-eminence.

N. B. Orders should express " *Hone's* Edition:"

Price 2s. 6d.

PROCEEDINGS IN AN ACTION

Between

The Rt. Hon. CHARLES J. FOX, Plaintiff,

and

JOHN HORNE TOOKE, *Esq.* Defendant.

A new edition.—This is perhaps the finest Specimen of Mr. Tooke's splendid talents.

In 8vo. Price 4s. 6d.

THE OCEAN CAVERN:

A Tale of the Tonga Isles. In Three Cantos.—The interesting story selected as the ground-work of this Poem, is in Mariner's Account of the Customs and Manners of the Inhabitants of the Tonga Islands. " The tale is beautifully related in the Poem, and occasions feelings which a real bard only can raise."

Printed by William Hone, 45, Ludgate Hill, London.

SELECTED TITLE PAGES AND ILLUSTRATIONS

THE
RIGHT DIVINE OF KINGS TO GOVERN WRONG!

Dedicated to the Holy Alliance

BY THE AUTHOR OF
THE POLITICAL HOUSE THAT JACK BUILT.

" The devil will not have me damn'd, lest the *oil* that is in me should set hell on fire."
SHAKSPEARE.

LONDON:
PRINTED FOR WILLIAM HONE,
45, LUDGATE-HILL.

1821.

Eighteenpence.

THE RIGHT DIVINE OF KINGS, &c.

No! HE has issued no such foul command,
But dooms down Despots by the People's hand;
Marks tyrants out for fall in every age,
Directs the justice of the people's rage;
And hurling vengeance on all royal crimes,
Ordains the REVOLUTIONS of the times!

A thing of no bowels————
———— from the crown to the toe, topfull
Of direst cruelty.—His Realm a slaughter-house—
The swords of soldiers are his teeth——
Iron for NAPLES, hid with English *gilt*.

SHAKSPEARE.

THE END.

Printed by W. Hone, Ludgate Hill, London.

A

SLAP AT SLOP

AND THE

Bridge-Street Gang.

BY THE AUTHOR OF THE

'POLITICAL HOUSE THAT JACK BUILT.'

With Twenty-seven Cuts.

LONDON:

PRINTED BY AND FOR WILLIAM HONE,

45, LUDGATE HILL.

1822.

Half-a-Crown.

" The Freeborn Englishman."

DR. SLOP'S OBSCENITY.

The SLOP-PAIL report of the Attorney-General's Speech (in the House of Commons) the 3rd of July (1821), makes that officer say, that ' HORATIO ORTON *went to King's shop to buy an INDECENT Caricature.*' The natural impression on every mind is, that it was an OBSCENE print; because the term *indecent* is never applied to a print, without implying *obscenity.* It was not only quite in character for *Slop*, who amused his readers with the *obscenity* of ' FRESH FIG-LEAVES FOR ADAM AND EVE,' but it suited his *purpose* as a Member of the BRIDGE-STREET GANG, to fix OBSCENITY upon a political caricature. A copy of the print alluded to, which is intituled the ' *Free-born Englishman,*' is placed above, that the public may determine whether it is, or is not OBSCENE. Every one who looks at it will naturally be astonished at the impudence of the imputation, and some perhaps be induced to call the utterer by that short but natural appellation which no honest man in society ever applied but to a miscreant, who ought to have it burnt in upon his forehead as a mark to avoid him by. A ' curtain ' before this print, to save SLOP from the infamy its appearance brands him with, would be more serviceable to him now, than, it is to be hoped, *his* ' CURTAIN BEFORE POTIPHAR'S WIFE ' was *amusing* to his readers.

The R----l FOWLS;

OR,

The Old Black Cock's

ATTEMPT

TO CROW OVER HIS ILLUSTRIOUS MATE.

A Poem.

By the AUTHOR *of the* R ——— L BROOD.

SEVENTH EDITION.

LONDON:

PRINTED FOR EFFINGHAM WILSON,

88, ROYAL EXCHANGE.

1820.

(Price One Shilling.)

" Be just, and fear not."

———

THIS IS

THE THING,

That will shortly correct

the *Scoundrels of Pelf*,

That would plunder

the WEALTH,

That supports the

LAWS OF ENGLAND.

"———— forth he goes,
Like to a harvest-man, that's task'd to mow
Or all, or lose his hire."

THIS IS

THE MAN,

That will execute well,

All who merit a *Rope*

That hangs on A THING,

That will shortly correct the *Scoundrels* of *Pelf*,

That would plunder *the* WEALTH,

That supports the LAWS OF ENGLAND.

SUPPORTING CHURCH AND STATE.

"Labourers in the Wineyard."

NOTES TO THE PAMPHLETS

The Political House that Jack built (Early December) 1819
I have described the impulse which started Hone on the composition of this pamphlet. The objective situation was an added stimulus. The Peterloo outrage had taken place in mid-August, and popular indignation was exacerbated by the Home Secretary's message to the Manchester magistrates, conveying to them 'the great satisfaction derived by His Royal Highness from their prompt, decisive and efficient measures for the preservation of the public tranquillity'.

Far from being preserved, the 'public tranquillity' was completely shattered by the news of the brutal attack by Yeomanry Cavalry on the peaceful crowd of unarmed men, women and children. Far from attempting to understand and placate this nation-wide indignation, the new session of Parliament which opened on 23 November scolded and threatened. The Address from the throne spoke of the necessity for the
utmost vigilance and exertion to check the dissemination of the doctrines of treason and impiety, and to impress upon the minds of all classes of his Majesty's subjects that it is from the cultivation of the principles of religion, and from a just subordination to lawful authority, that we can alone expect the continuance of that Divine favour and protection which have hitherto been so signally experienced in this kingdom.

Six Bills were immediately brought forward, all restrictive of ancient rights, and two of them curtailing still further the free expression and circulation of opinion on public matters.

Page 35
Wellington throws his sword into the scale-pan, laden with scrolls typifying three legal abuses, yet out-weighed by the quill pen.

Page 38
The Temple of the Constitution, surmounted by the figure of Liberty holding a staff topped by the *bonnet rouge*, adopted from the French revolutionaries.

Page 40
The 'Vermin'. From left to right: a court functionary with wand of office, a cavalry officer in exotic uniform, a clerical magistrate, a tax-collector, and a Crown lawyer.

Page 41
The printing press, as the most effective weapon in the defence of freedom; a favourite symbol, always carefully delineated, of Cruikshank's.

Page 42
Robert Gifford, Attorney-General. As the initiator of prosecutions for political offences he aroused wide animosity by the abuse of his powers.

There were 33 informations in 1819 against printers and booksellers for political libel, but only one-third were prosecuted to conviction.

Page 44
The Prince Regent (he became George IV a few weeks after this was published). His boots and peacock feathers continued to symbolise traits of his character as read by a hostile public. Note the corkscrew amongst 'the august orders round his waistband.

Page 45
'And, when Britain's in tears, /sails about at his pleasure' is a specific reference to the fact that at the time of Peterloo and after, the Regent was at Brighton with the barge the *Royal George* and his yacht, in which he attended the Cowes regatta.

The 'Friends of his youth' refers to a group of more progressive Whigs, especially Charles James Fox (by then dead), Sheridan, Erskine, Grey and others. They had been jettisoned in 1811 when the Prince chose to retain Perceval as head of the first Administration of his Regency.

Page 48
'The Guilty Trio'. On the left is Henry Addington, Lord Sidmouth, then Home Secretary—hence his constable's staff. His title of 'Doctor' and the enema bag derive from his father's profession, who was a physician before becoming a politician and Prime Minister. The 'Circular' which brought him fame was one of many which he wrote to zealous magistrates who apprehended pedlars or petty shop-keepers who might be found carrying a radical publication. Castlereagh, in the centre and suave as usual, carries the cat o' nine tails associated with his early career in his native Ireland, the 'Land of mis-rule'. The triangle was used for flogging and half-hanging, forms of persecution which he did not reprehend strongly enough to satisfy popular taste. As Britain's plenipotentiary at the post-war meetings of the continental powers, he was acquiescent in the restoration of absolutist regimes. Foreign Secretary Canning, on the right, was widely regarded as a bit of a bounder in his own set, and also with distrust. His flippancy was irresponsible, and sometimes cruel without being witty. His reference to 'the revered and ruptured Ogden' embittered the Reformers, and was strongly criticised by Tom Moore. Ogden was a Manchester printer and leading reformer, who was fettered whilst in jail for months, though seventy years old and suffering from severe hernia. These three are identified at some length, as they often turn up. Another favourite target was Wellington, suspected of a preference for militaristic methods, and recently taken into the Cabinet.

The Real or Constitutional House that Jack built (December) 1819
A quick riposte, but lacking in penetrative power. Artist not known.

Page 65
The Pilot is William Pitt the Younger and the line is from a poem by Canning. The argument harks back to the political rivalries of 1806–7.

Page 69
The team now introduced balances the Parliamentary characters described previously; demons or heroes, according to which way you are

facing. Major Cartright, the veteran Reform leader; T. J. Wooler, transmogrified as usual into the symbol of his journal *The Black Dwarf*; Sir Francis Burdett, Bart.; Henry Hunt, popular leader and flamboyant orator, who launched a scheme for collecting money by which Reformers might buy up the rotten boroughs. Others are not certainly identifiable as individuals, but will stand for those named in the text.

Page 72
Cobbett had just returned from America, where he had sought refuge on the suspension of Habeas Corpus in 1817. He had promised to bring back Thomas Paine's earthly remains, a rash undertaking which he fulfilled in the letter but neglected thereafter.

He denied that his debt to Burdett was a personal obligation, holding that the money had been advanced and expended for common political ends.

Page 80
This counter to the Clerical Magistrate in Cruikshank's satire is identified by Dr. George as Rowland Hill, an itinerant preacher who was refused priest's orders because of his preaching in the open air.

The Man in the Moon (January) 1820
The opening, major section is a pretty faithful parody of the Address from the throne at the opening of Parliament the previous November. By the end of December the Six Bills referred to previously had received the Royal assent and were popularly known as the Gagging Acts. There is little that needs elucidation in this very succint satire.

Page 92
Johnny Moon Calf is clearly the lunar variant of John Bull.

Page 94
Steel Lozenges were a popular nostrum: 'Aromatic Lozenges of Steel' was the alluring name of one brand.

Page 95
Although Britain disowned all connivance with the Continental Powers in their restoring the principles of absolutism and religious intolerance in the 'liberated' states, reports of numerous atrocities reduced the value of such assurances.

Page 96
'Little Books' referred to the radical penny or twopenny tracts, which after the new Act might not be sold for less than sixpence.

A Political Christmas Carol, Page 102
The rats beside Castlereagh are a fawning Attorney-General and a pensive Solicitor-General, Gifford and Copley, to whom Castlereagh had addressed the injunction
> Go draw your quills, and draw six Bills . . .
Copley is pensive because of the shame his action will bring on his father's memory.

'*The Doctor*' *Page 104*
The reference to the *Beggar's Opera* would have been readily taken by everyone.

The Loyal Man in the Moon (February) 1820
This shows the author of our second item in sprightlier mood, though certainly no less loyal. It does not follow Hone's original closely, being roughly concerned with the approaching election at Westminster, the constituency where Radical strength could most . irely be gauged, as it had an unusually democratic franchise. Artist not identified.

Page 107
The place of the Regent on Hone's title-page is taken by Henry Hunt.

Page 112
Lord Fitzwilliam had been removed as Lord Lieutenant, for allowing a meeting of Yorkshire freeholders to pass a resolution asking for an enquiry into the events at Peterloo.

Page 116
Burdett, Hunt, Hobhouse, Thelwall (just visible), Gale Jones the orator, and Cobbett, the chins of the last two touching. Wooler is black, of course. The shadowy profile top left may be Francis Place. Burdett and Hobhouse were the Reform candidates for Westminster.

Page 119
A gibe at the ineffectual survivors of the Broad-bottom administration of 1805–7, led by Thomas Erskine, ex-Lord Chancellor.

Page 121
Cobbett, as the Hampshire Hog, with Paine's skeleton, followed by Hunt with a begging sack.

Page 124
Major Cartwright, wearing the white top hat of a Hunt-ite.

Page 128
From line 15 down to line 14 on the next page, a long and mendacious diatribe against Hone.

Page 133
King George had died on 29 January.

*The Political '*A, Apple-Pie*'* (January) 1820
Ammunition for the Reformers' cause was provided by investigation of the numerous offices ('places' or 'jobs'), whose occupants were appointed by various Ministers, thus serving as rewards for, or encouraging towards, voting in the direction indicated by the source of the bounty. These sinecures, for most of them carried only nominal duties, had long been a scandal, but their extent and incidence had not been investigated fully until the publication of the *Extraordinary Red Book* or, more exhaustively, in John Wade's *Black Book, or Corruption Unmasked*. This was sold

cheaply in parts, and amounted to 840 pages when complete. There were two *Apple-Pies* published within a few weeks of each other; the one chosen has the greater number of cuts, all by G. Cruickshank. Below is an extract from the *Black Book:*

A Classification of Placemen, Pensioners, &c. with their Yearly Allowances

Number of Persons		Yearly Sum				Total
		£		£		£
251 have	..	50 to	..	60	..	13,038
68	..	60	..	70	..	4,242
58	..	70	..	80	..	4,246
15	..	80	..	90	..	1,213
32	..	90	..	100	..	2,962
540	..	100	..	200	..	63,826
266	..	200	..	300	..	57,598
194	..	300	..	400	..	61,568
110	..	400	..	500	..	45,507
131	..	500	..	600	..	77,068
76	..	600	..	700	..	46,563
35	..	700	..	800	..	25,819
41	..	800	..	900	..	33,013
20	..	900	..	1,000	..	18,688
234	..	1,000	..	2,000	..	304,657
97	..	2,000	..	3,000	..	217,118
49	..	3,000	..	4,000	..	156,778
33	..	4,000	..	5,000	..	140,263
17	..	5,000	..	6,000	..	89,066
13	..	6,000	..	7,000	..	82,817
11	..	7,000	..	8,000	..	81,128
7	..	8,000	..	9,000	..	58,254
6	..	9,000	..	10,000	..	54,756
25	..	10,000	..	20,000	..	349,581
7	..	20,000	..	30,000	..	181,686
6	..	30 000	..	40,000	..	197,479
2	..	50,000	..	and upwards	..	100,631

2,344 Persons receive annually £2,474,805

The Queen's Matrimonial Ladder (Early August) 1820

The return of Queen Caroline and the almost immediate introduction into the House of Lords of a Bill of Pains and Penalties against her transformed the political scene. The Bill alleged unseemly conduct by the Queen, even amounting to adulterous intercourse, the documentary evidence for which was contained in a green bag. Evidence could be called on both sides and a number of Italians, some of whom had been in the Queen's service, had been brought over by the Government, in the expectation that their evidence would tell against the Queen. It was widely believed that they had been bribed, and the populace regarded them with violent hostility.

If it were not confirmed from less partial sources, one would have believed that the caricaturists had invented the whole farcical masquerade of the Queen's arraignment. There is little point in moralising the situation. The Princess and her daughter were destined to be pawns in the struggle between political factions.

Hone's tract gives a plausible and emotionally effective version of the deterioration of the Royal relationship. The pamphlet was issued before the start of the hearing in the Lords on 17 August.

'Non Mi Ricordo!' (September)1820

One of the key Italian witnesses, Majocchi, became famous overnight, having developed a defective memory, though the lapses occurred only at certain crucial episodes in his testimony. As realisation of the at least eccentric behaviour of the Princess on her travels began to spread, it became necessary to intensify the partisanship of the Queen's supporters.

The pillorying of the King is really quite irrelevant, but the squib has some amusing passages, especially about the conspiracy among the clocks, which guys Sidmouth's propensity to discover plots everywhere.

The Radical Ladder; or, Hone's Political Ladder and his Non Mi Ricordo Explained and Applied (October) 1820

This is the only really comprehensive retort to the Radical case, and chosen for that reason, even though its technique is conventional. Cruikshank was seduced to supply the frontispiece, which lends some support to the widely stated assertion that he could never bear to turn down a commission. Certainly, he was in sore need of placating the authorities, for some of the cruellest shafts at the Regent (and King) were his. This 'radical ladder' of his does not traduce the Queen in person, only her being used as a stalking-horse by the extremists, which was broadly true. And Cruikshank had often earlier expressed his distaste for demagogic firebrands. But he thoroughly identified with Reform in its humanitarian aspects, and with the defence of Press freedom.

The Loyalists were fortunate in receiving even a minimum of co-operation from him, for they were more scantily supplied with artistic than with literary henchmen. But they got little else out of him.

Pathetic evidence of the absence of public enthusiasm for their productions is supplied by a note to The Radical Chiefs, a Mock-Heroic Poem, published in mid-1821, with a frontispiece by I. R. Cruikshank. The promoter of this riposte sees nothing to cheer him in the campaign which had by then been raging for eighteen months:

Such was the apathy and ingratitude of the loyal party to their friends, that from the government downwards, scarcely a purchaser or a patron could be found. That at this period Hone, of Ludgate Hill, the Radical pamphlet seller, sold forty thousand copies of anti-Loyal publications: whilst Asperne could scarcely sell a thousand.

The New Pilgrim's Progress (October) 1820

This little piece introduces a new measure of scurrility into the contest which could hardly fail to be exploited. The verbatim evidence does lend credence to the existence of a state of easy intimacy in the Princess's household.

The pivot to the case was Bartolommeo Bergami, the Italian engaged by the Princess as Courier, and soon promoted to be her Chamberlain. He was a handsome fellow, with fine whiskers, and very popular it is said with the London populace, though they never saw him as he did not land here. Perhaps they reckoned that he had given Caroline a better deal than her husband had.

She secured from the Emperor of Austria an Order of Chivalry for him, and herself instituted the Order of St. Caroline, of which she made Bergami Grand Master. The incidents depicted can all be authenticated from the evidence of witnesses.

The verses might have come from the pages of John Bull, which had recently appeared under the gifted and not squeamish editorship of Theodore Hook. Artist not identified.

The Political Showman—at Home! (April) 1821
There were two major pamphlets this year by the now veteran collaborators. This is the earliest of them; a synthesis of all the evil organisms that pullulate in the dark repression of an autocratic system. It is the most philosophic of Hone's pieces, and Cruikshank has raised his inspiration to the highest level. I would say that the seven-headed monster on the title-page is amongst the finest cuts he ever did.

The 'Showman' is a humanised printing press: the 'Legitimate Vampire', the last exhibit, is to be destroyed by the power of the Word, 'accelerated by the powerful exhibition of the Wood-Draughts'. This is almost certainly the pamphlet announced earlier by Hone as 'The Triumph of the Press'. The change of title was much for the better.

Most of the creatures are easily identifiable:

Bags: Eldon, Lord Chancellor
A Crocodile: Sir John Leech, Vice-Chancellor. Hated as Chairman of the Milan Commission, which gathered evidence against Princess Caroline.
The Locust: the Bishops
A Scorpion: Wellington
The Lobster: the Military
A Prime Crutch: Lord Liverpool, a nincompoop of a Prime Minister
The Opossum: a borough-monger
Black Rats: Crown Lawyers
A Cadge Anchor: The Duke of Clarence, like all the Royal Dukes, a money-sucker
A Water Scorpion: George IV
Dirkpatrick: Castlereagh—note the bleeding shamrock
The Bloodhound: torments Ireland and also Spain
The Doctor: Sidmouth once more
The Booby: a sinecurist
A Twopenny Flat: a lump of tallow with a wick, stuck on a cobbler's or any poor worker's stall or bench
The Slop Pail: The New Times, Dr. Stoddart's daily dish of ultra-Royalist propaganda
My Eye: the apotheosis of the printing press
The Legitimate Vampire: returns the argument to its commencement, the

hydra creature on the title-page. Hone stresses, that it is the European system which is paranoiac, not merely the British.

From *The Right Divine of Kings to Govern Wrong!* (March) 1821
This is a partial revision of the *Jure Divino* written by Daniel Defoe in 1706. It was written

to expose this destructive doctrine [of passive obedience and non-resistance], and disentangle the threads so artfully twisted into snares for the unwary by priestcraft. The Jure Divino *is defective in arrangement and versification. . . . The present is an attempt to separate the gold from the dross. . . . It is a forcible and argumentative satire against the nonsense from hole-and-corner and lawnsleeve men . . .*

There is another reason for publishing this satire, besides the revival of Priestcraft. Its twin brother is alive. Kingcraft rears up its terrific mass, muffled in the mantle of Legitimacy; its head cowled and crowned, and dripping with the oil of Divine Rights; its eyes glaring deadly hate to human happiness; its lips demanding worship for itself . . .

The pamphlet called forth two of the most magnificent of Cruikshank's designs. The first clearly derives from the passage quoted above, which itself derives from Hazlitt's tirades against Legitimacy. But 'The wood-cut at the end', wrote the *Examiner*, 'a personification of Royalty in its excess, is still more striking. It is Spenser's Iron Man brought forward in his real character'. It was also perhaps suggested by some of the prints in Hone's collection, for instance Hollar's 'The Patenty', where the man is 'emblemised' by the implements of his social essence.

From *A Slap at Slop and the Bridge-Street Gang* (August) 1821
This was the last and lengthiest of the Hone–Cruikshank squibs. It was originally issued in newspaper format, with a banner-head imitating that of *The New Times*. This daily paper was launched by Dr. John Stoddard after he had been dismissed from *The Times* for persistently ignoring editorial directives. *The New Times* was Government subsidised and the mouth-piece of an ultra-Royalist policy. All editions of the *Slap* after Queen Caroline's death carried an extra woodcut at the head of the first column, with the text beginning 'Her Majesty died by the dagger of Persecution'.

In 1822 Hone re-issued the *Slap* in pamphlet form, at popular request, but protesting at the bad taste that forced him to do so. Certainly, it loses something of its style in the more compact form, particularly the three large blocks by Cruikshank which extended across the column. The pamphlet runs to 56 pages and there are 27 woodcuts. It seems that Hone wished to obliterate once and for all the reputation of the ex-Jacobin and sycophant Stoddard.

The Constitutional Association, founded in December 1820, was intended to carry on the struggle against seditious and immoral publications which the Attorney-General neglected to prosecute. It was soon discredited, though some unlucky Radicals spent time in custody through their informations.

A large part of the paper is taken up with mock-advertisements written by Hone with comic ingenuity. Though both the collaborators' talents are lavishly displayed, this is the pamphlet which can best be spared under the present limitations of space. The interest of its subject is limited, belonging to the minutiae of literary history. We have chosen two specimens, with great difficulty, as all clamour for revival.

This was the last satire that Hone produced. In 1822 he collected remaining stocks and made up a volume entitled *Facetiae and Miscellanies*, with a mock-modest Preface. This was not issued until 1827, and then under the imprint of a different publisher.

From *The R---l Fowls*

Title-page of a verse satire, not otherwise illustrated, by Isaac Robert Cruikshank, elder brother of George by two years. The King menaces the Queen's defenders, Brougham and Denman. Sidmouth, Castlereagh, Eldon and Liverpool look on anxiously.

From *The Loyalist House that Jack built*

A double-page spread from a lumpen production, of interest for its un-inhibited expression of a preference for drastic measures for maintaining 'law and order'. A little before the Cato Street disaster, it is enough to set off a suspicion that even then some persons might have known that it was going to happen, or was likely to happen, soon. Artist not known.

From *First Book for the Instruction of Students in the King's College*

The foundation of a University of London was adumbrated amongst a group of Whigs and 'philosophic' Radicals, Dissenters or even freethinkers. The intention was, besides the usual function of a university, to break the doctrinal monopoly of the Church of England imposed on the existing universities. This idea took material form in University College, Gower Street, opened in 1829.

Tory and other interests riposted by founding, with the support of George IV, a college on the traditional Church of England principles, which became King's College in the Strand, opened in 1832.

The young artist Robert Seymour drew some plates for two pamphlets very much in the Hone manner, whose satire was aimed against any attempt to hold back the secularisation of higher education.

Seymour has created a splendid tribute to the achievements of these earlier caricatures, grouping together the entire membership of the Radical demonology in support of their tottering structure, a brilliant mockery of the survivals of a savage age.